THE REAL IRAQ WAR

THE
REAL IRAQ WAR

*As Told by an on-the-scene U.S. Army
Intelligence Officer*

Intelligence Officer, Mr. A.

ADVOCATE HOUSE
Sarasota Florida

For information regarding permissions, write to:
A Cappela Publishing
P.O. Box 3691
Sarasota FL 34230-3691

Library of Congress Cataloging-in-Publication Data
Mr. A.
The Real Iraq War As Told by an on-the-scene U.S. Army Intelligence Officer / Mr. A.
p.   cm.
978-0-9818933-3-4 PB
1. War. 2.Religion 3. History 4. Social Science

First Edition

Printed in Canada

Design by Carol Tornatore

ACKNOWLEDGMENTS

Gratitude to the countless women and men of the Washington Brigade (who cannot be named without compromising their operational security) for their honesty and guidance, their commitment to the truth and love of country; for their protection which kept me and the team members alive.

Gratitude to the intelligence detatchment of California Army National Guard for their comradely spirit, their commitment to hard work and suffering, and to their fulfillment to duty and beyond. To my special friend, 1st Lieutenant Burbank (not his real name for his protection), and to all those who are very special to me: to the patrol officers and police officers and to those who cried when we lost 1st Lieutenant Travis (not his real name).

Gratitude to all officers and enlisted men of the brave Marine expeditionary units that fought the Fallujah War 2004, especially those who were stationed in the Death Triangle. To my heroes whose pictures appear in this book. You have a special moment in my heart and soul. We faced the fear together and we faced the victory together.

Gratitude to my wife who encouraged me to write my memoirs and turn them into a book.

My special gratitude to Ula, of Georgia State University in Augusta, who helped me edit the manuscript.

My special gratitude to all my publishers and editors. I thank you all for your true commitment to the good.

May God bless you all and bless America, land of the brave and the free.

SPECIAL ACKNOWLEDGMENT
TO MY BEST FRIEND
1ST LIEUTENANT BURBANK

In life, we meet people who seem very ordinary. They don't mean a lot to us in the begining until they engrave their memory in our hearts and minds. We walk with them, we eat with them, we share casual moments with them. We drive around together, we laugh together, and at the end of the day, we say goodbye.

Later, we feel something different about one another. The reasons are many: a shared situation: this one stands by you; that one asks you how you feel when you are down; or somebody asks about you when you are not there . . . little things but that caused us to reevaluate our hidden assumptions.

Later, we realize who is true and who is only someone to remember. In the war, each relationship is tested to the max. There is no faking or pretending.

Therefore, my friend Burbank, I will never forget the moment when you came running, ten minutes before the plane was to take off from the airport in Orlando, Florida, to look for me. The flight held over one hundred seventy troops, yet even the mission commander did not come to see us off.

But you did.

It meant more than a lot to me.

I met you outside, on my way to the flight, but I admired you, I appreciated your courage and commitment to a true friend.

I am honored to know a noble person like you. You have my friendship until the day I die.

Your friend,
Mr. A.

CONTENTS

1

BOOTS ON THE GROUND:
FEBRUARY, 2004

We arrived at the Baghdad International Airport (BIAP) at 8 P.M. Everything was pitch black. There was no light and no movement except from the two people standing next to the rear of the plane directing us to walk quickly to the assembly area behind a huge tent, which was far away. When we reached the assembly area we saw that it was an open space with a few cones that formed a small path to direct traffic. I saw a tall 1st Sergeant waiting for us in the dark, holding nothing other than a dim, red light.

There were twenty-six of us: Intelligence Interrogators and Counterintelligence Agents who were only beginning to get the real idea about the gravity of the situation. We started walking toward the 1st Sergeant in single file, one behind the other. Each of us had two duffel bags strapped on: one on the front of our bodies and the other strapped to our backs. We carried no rifles or pistols. Silently, we walked in the dark until we reached the 1st Sergeant.

Next to the 1st Sergeant stood three armed troops, each with his rifle slung across his shoulder. Pistols were strapped on their right hips, just above their knees. Two army trucks were parked in front of us with their rear doors opened, and three other trucks were behind the 1st Sergeant, each with its rear door open as well. Far away, above the trees, I saw lights glittering in the dark. I knew that we were quite a distance from the city. I could feel the soldiers breathing heavily because of the weight of their loads. I did not hear a single word until the 1st Sergeant spoke.

He immediately started giving instructions like every 1st Sergeant does. I will never forget what he said: "Listen up, fine people. Welcome to Iraq. I want you to load all your gear on those two trucks behind me, and each one of you find a seat on those other three trucks. No smoking, no talking, and no use of light. We do this as quiet as a hunting coyote." At that point, I realized that we had entered the death alley. We must pay attention or die.

The three troops who had come with the 1st Sergeant climbed on the first truck, the one parked to their left. They asked us to unload our duffel bags and hand them over to be loaded onto the truck. Everyone began to unload his cargo onto the ground. The three troops picked it up again, piece by piece, to be loaded nicely and neatly onto the truck. In a few minutes the truck was full.

The three soldiers came down and locked the truck,

securing it before they climbed onto the second truck, closing and securing the doors. Two of the soldiers got on one truck, and the third got on the other. Each of us had to find a seat on one of the three trucks, and we had to do it without uttering a single word.

The 1st Sergeant jumped into the driver's seat of one of the trucks and the convoy proceeded to the Baghdad International Airport Army Base.

Twenty minutes later, we arrived at our destination. We dismounted and stood in line at the 1st Sergeant's instruction, waiting to have our linens issued. One by one we entered a little building with two doors. The building stood far away from Saddam's sons' palaces, which were partially damaged from the strike fighters' bombing during the liberation of Iraq.

We found one civilian inside. He worked for KBR, Kellogg, Brown and Root, a civilian company that contracted with the Army to provide catering services. He issued each of us two wool blankets and a pillow. When a person left the room, the 1st Sergeant told him the number of the green tent he should spend the night in.

All the tents were alike. The city of tents was confusing, but the civilian helped us a lot. The Army's red flashlight came in handy, too.

The tents had no protection other than some sandbags around them; their roofs were not protected, so mortar rounds could come right through.

I was very tired and so was everyone else. I had an idea about how vulnerable we were, but I did not bother worrying about mortar rounds or Katusha rockets that first night — I just wanted to go to sleep. Lieutenant Travis the "ghost rider," had told me that he wanted to take a shower and I just told him "good luck." I had taken mine before the flight.

At 6 A.M. Lieutenant Travis McLoud and I were fully dressed. We went to the dining facility to have our breakfast. It was a huge tent made to accommodate six hundred people at a time. The food was good: there were all varieties of fruits, eggs, milk, bacon, etc. We ate gratefully and left to go to the Brigade Command meeting.

We entered a medium-sized room in Udai Saddam Hussein's palace to have the war briefing. CW3 (Chief Warrant Officer 3) "Jack" was standing next to his podium, greeting every person who entered the room with a big, happy smile on his face. Every person greeted him back and found a place to sit. When we were all situated, Jack began his briefing. He talked about the differences in cultures we would encounter. Then he talked about what the Brigade Command expected from us. He advised us to be extremely careful and to pay great attention to details. The briefing was scheduled to last one hour, but it continued for four. Everyone in the room got the picture: the Command depended on intelligence personnel for accurate reports and made their decisions about the war based upon this information; therefore, we depended on our informants to be accurate.

I saw the interrogators' and the counterintelligence agents' faces and their body language . . . their wounded eyes and their fake smiles. I also saw their fear.

A second after the CW3 was finished talking, I found myself surrounded by these fearful men. They asked me many questions about the culture again. The most important question was what would they do if they had a female informant?

Women in the Arabian culture are very important in many ways; however, they are also put down in many ways as well. The question was valid. Many situations could create the possibility of dealing with a female informant, and they would have to be handled carefully.

Generally, a family did not allow an Arab woman to work unless they desperately needed the money. Even if the woman's job was near her home and she was paid well and her job was decent and respectable, if her work required her to be alone with any of her coworkers, the family would ask her to leave the job. The family's honor would always override their economic need. So if she refused to leave her job, she would be killed. This was problematic because interrogators require privacy. They need to be alone with their informants for many reasons, including the nature of the information, and most importantly, for the safety of the informant.

The nature of the agent's job makes it totally unwelcome by the culture in regards to its women.

I told my fellow Intel folks that I did not recommend a woman informant, but if they had to talk to one, I suggested that they look for a woman dressed in modern, Western clothes with a scarf on her head, (a sign of respect in their culture); one who was not in the traditional long black gown that coverd her from head to toe, her face covered with a veil. Sometimes these women concealed guns under their gowns, and they were not usually flattered by our goal of saving Iraq.

I told them that even though there might be some young,

modern Arab girls willing to help and be informants, They should look for older and more mature women. Still, even with these precautions, meeting with them alone could be a fatal mistake for all parties involved.

We barely had time to eat lunch. We returned at 1 P.M. and found the 1st Sergeant patiently waiting to tell us the last of the instructions about traveling to the final war-post destination. The previous night he had told us that we would be transported outside Baghdad to Babylon after lunch. I was assigned to be a team leader in Babylon. I was excited to finally get to see where Babylonian kings and queens had lived, and I was also excited to see the place where the biblical stories had taken place.

My excitement about Babylon did not last too long, however. I loaded my luggage and equipment on the truck to go to Babylon. I was sitting on my duffel bag in the truck, talking to my friend 1st Lieutenant Burbank, when I heard the Major calling my name. I stood up and waved at the major. She walked toward me with a big, happy smile and smart, bright eyes. I knew that something was not quite right, but I did not know exactly what it was.

The Major told me that there had been a mistake in the language coding. I asked her what was wrong with the codes, and the major replied that I could not go to Babylon because I did not speak Farsi. I told the Major that she was right, that I could not speak Farsi, and she told me that I was needed in the central command in Baghdad; that a native Arabic speaking team leader position was available for me and that I needed to unload my equipment immediately. I was needed for troop protection in the Baghdad International Airport.

I had mixed feelings about the decision. I was supposed to go to Babylon with my friends, with people I had been with for the past three months. We had gone through training together and understood each other very well. We cared for one another like brothers and sisters since we were from the same unit back home. Leaving them meant starting all over again with a new group of people. I would have to deal with personality conflicts and all the other issues surrounding a new group. It was hard for all of us.

All those who were in the truck stood up to help me extract my duffel bags and other items from the truck and helped me move them to another truck which the major had sent for that purpose. When everything was moved, I turned around and saluted them all and said, "Goodbye, my best friends, and good luck to all of you."

The entire group said their goodbyes to me and I began to leave, but my friend Burbank started singing a song we always sang for fun: *Marhaba ya Marhaba*. (Welcome Oh yes you welcome). I stood and turned back and sang the song with them all. It was emotional, and I knew that Burbank wanted to make the moment into something better than it was. He did not like seeing me separated from the group because I was the man that he trusted as his friend, mate, and Arabic linguist. I had promised them back at Fort Hood that I would teach them Arabic in Iraq, but instead, my best friends left to go to their destinations, and I went to the brigade headquarters.

I followed the major, wondering where I was going. We entered the office and I saw a lot of happy faces awaiting my arrival. I was welcomed again and again by my brigade commander and company commander.

I sat with the company commander and the First Sergeant while both explained my assignment. My team would be responsible for gathering intelligence for maneuvering units that were assigned to protect the base. The primary purpose would be the protection of the troops. Later I was introduced to all the commanders of the companies that involved troop protection and also to the commanding general. They introduced me to the members of my team and to a civilian dignitary security company that provided protection to Iraqi transitional government administrative members.

My first day was spent getting to know key personnel and my direct contact in case I needed help with official business. Unfortunately, I was unable to meet the base mayor — the most important administrative officer — who was not available. I wanted to meet him and become his friend, or at least become *known* to him.

The next day, I assumed my duty. I took my team and went with the rest to meet the former interrogator's team leader, to be shown around and given a real life experience. We were all glad to have arrived safely and to begin our first day of work. We met the team leader in his office. He had a happy face and the largest smile his lips could handle. He was standing alone in a huge, empty room that used to be an interrogation room for Saddam's enemies. Steel bars stretched from one side of the room to the other, and rings that once had held chains were still on the bars. It looked like a slaughter house that once had held sides of beef. A Russian AK-47 was lying on the ground on the far side of the room. Boxes of papers were everywhere, and a few foam mattresses were folded and placed against the wall.

The team leader shook hands with each of us. We noticed his excitement and asked him, "Why are you so happy today?"

He replied that his replacement had arrived and that he would be going home the next day! Of course, we were also happy for him, that he had made it to this day alive. We would carry the flag from here and meet the challenges.

I asked him where the other team members were, and he said he had instructed them to go pack since we had already arrived. What nice guys — they didn't even want to see who was replacing them!

I asked what I should do for starters, what he wanted from me, what I should and should not do, and so forth. He answered that there was not enough time, and that he was not prepared for a big speech, but that he would take us to the base command the next day and would take us for a tour around the base.

I took my team back and told them to go and arrange their living quarters — to set up their sleeping areas, empty their duffel bags — anything to make the situation more livable. We were all stationed in a big, concrete building that formerly housed Saddam's special guard. It was a fort, and it was the safest shelter I had had in three months. So we all fixed our living quarters and took the rest of the day off. I told them to go and sleep, since we had not rested from the moment we had left Kuwait earlier.

In the morning we packed into our Army truck and went

to breakfast at 6 A.M. At 7 A.M. we were in company formation for accountability. By 8 A.M. we were in the former interrogators team leader's office. He welcomed us and immediately took us to meet the command of the Base Troop Protection Leadership.

We met a very hospitable group of leaders. We had tea and coffee and introduced ourselves one by one and talked about the U.S. and Iraq and about protecting the troops. All the commanders were very excited to find out that I was a native. Their happiness was such that I felt welcomed, even at the most difficult moment of my life. I knew their expectations were very high, but they had met me now, and I knew that I would meet — and exceed — their expectations. I knew my capabilities, and sure enough, three weeks later I had accomplished everything they had wanted from me and more.

We had finished the meeting with the Base Security Command and the former interrogators team leader took us for a tour around the perimeters of the base. He showed us the routes to go to the Green Zone and some of his sources' houses. That was the last time we heard from him.

The next day, after the company formation, the third team leader asked us to take him on a tour to introduce him to the local Iraqi informants and show him the routes to the Green Zone. We asked the command for permission to take the trip, and all the troops stood ready in their battle dress uniforms.

Each of them wore a bullet-proof vest. M16's were slung across their chests and pistols were tied in holsters, just above their knees.

I was the only one with my pistol clipped to the bullet-proof vest on my chest.

Three HMMWVs (High Mobility Multi-Purpose Wide Vehicles) were fully fueled, each with a long range machine gun mounted on its roof.

The second team leader had volunteered to lead the convoy. He had been with us the previous day when the former interrogators teams took us on our tour. The third team had positioned themselves in the middle and my team secured the convoy at the rear.

The convoy commander had double checked his mission confirmation with the company command and ordered the convoy to move. After a few minutes we exited the base from the East gate and merged onto a very narrow paved alley. The right side of the alley was bordered with a wall about nine yards high. The left side was fenced with tall grass that grew from the irrigation canal which had not been maintained since the first day of Iraq's liberation. Water was flowing uncontrol-ably across the narrow, paved road. We drove slowly through the running water, and soon passed a huge mosque on the left edge of the alley.

We turned onto another narrow asphalt road and passed a few gypsy tents on our right. Three hundred yards further, the convoy commander screamed into the radio to stop the convoy. We hit the brakes and immediately prepared to engage the enemy. A second later, the commander ordered us to reverse one hundred yards. He called on his radio for me to walk to his vehicle to speak to him.

I ran toward him with the dreadful feeling that something was wrong. I was running with my weapon in the defensive position, a round in its chamber. I was breathing heavily when I reached him because I had been running fast and my nerves were on edge.

He told me that he had seen a road bomb on the right side of the road and he wanted me to ask the locals whether or not they knew who had planted it. We had come along the same road the previous day and there had been no bomb.

He ordered the convoy to dismount and conduct security around the three vehicles while he radioed the base. Next, he radioed the EOD (Explosives and Ordinates) guys to detonate the bomb or carry it away to be dismantled.

We all went, one by one, to see the road bomb for the very first time. It was only our second day in Iraq. Each of us felt completely vulnerable, as if we could die at any moment.

All of the local Iraqis said that they hadn't seen who had planted the bomb intended to kill us.

EOD came dressed like space men. Each wore a huge glass helmet, heavy body armor and heavily armored pants. Each carried a device in one hand and a briefcase in the other. They ordered us to back off a hundred yards or more. We did so, scattering to protect them from any attack that might occur while they worked.

EOD dug the bomb out. It contained two 82mm mortar rounds, ready to go off by the attached trip wire. We were all happy that the second team leader had seen it — we could have lost the whole team on our second day in Iraq had he not. God's grace made it the first and last major threat for team number two until they returned home, but this was not the case with my team.

2

REALITY CHECK:
END OF FEBRUARY, 2004

Usually, when a person from the Army takes the lead, he or she will go through phases in the mission progress. This starts with the Crawling Phase, which is establishing your preliminary necessities for your work. Then comes the Walking Phase, which governs a clear understanding of what you have on your hands, utilizing your resources to carry out your mission to the fullest. Last comes the Running Phase, in which you are on the ball, mastering the use of every moment of training, your equipment, and your personnel's expertise to carry out the mission. Intelligence collection is not a joke; it is not an accidental or random process that gives you a numerical result. Intelligence collection requires special equipment installed in a certain place, and it needs a system that works with us operating that system perfectly, in a timely manner. I was not lucky enough to have the privilege of completing the three phases to start my high speed mission. I had started in the Running Phase with only a pen and paper. No computer. No office. And in a short while I was to have no team. I was left alone, responsible for protecting the entire base and its troops. I said to myself, *hello, welcome to reality!*

I know for a fact that reality and theory are not alike. The two junior officers who were in charge of protecting the base were not communicating fully with each other. It was clear they were having a conflict that boiled down to their clashing personalities. The junior officer in charge of base protection had told our junior officer to let him know if she needed the office for the interrogators so he could talk to the mayor so that we could keep the office. Our junior officer ignored his words, which caused so many problems that it brought down the morale of the entire group. The Base Mayor gave the office to the MAPS (Maps and Graphics) personnel, so we lost the best location in the most secure building. My problems were just beginning!

Due to the confidentiality of my work, I tried to operate in a little space in the company office. The headquarters' office was already loaded; there were five teams in it, each operating different functions. My work was completely different, and I needed total privacy to complete it. It was impossible for me to operate out of the headquarters' office.

After three days, I came to a stop. I spoke to the commander face to face and explained to him what an interrogator needs. I was attached to an Operation Battalion, and their work was different from the Human Intelligence Battalion work. I broke down my work step by step, explaining what I needed in order to perform my job.

I told the commander that I could not allow the element that I wanted to discuss with him to enter the secured area, which could be exploited. I needed a place with one table and two chairs, someplace near the gate, where the area was not secured, and I needed it immediately.

The Commander personally went and talked to the mayor's staff. Two days later, the Mayor gave me an office: a trailer with no electricity. How could I do anything in a trailer with no electricity? How could I operate computers or establish relationships with the local people or meet informants in such a place with no air-conditioning? My first week was over, and I had done very little. My team members were wondering what to do. The commander told me to hook up some equipment and then wait a few days because the mayor would provide us with some generators. The trailer was too hot; team morale was plunging because they were not able to perform their duties. They had no translators. I told them to be patient and asked them to set up the equipment, which took two days to hook up. The trailer was far too small for two teams, and it was a great inconvenience for everyone. There was no walkway between desks, making it uncomfortable and nearly impossible to work.

Again, I went to the commander and sat down with him. I told him about our situation, and he returned to the mayor once again. The mayor's team then gave us a bigger trailer, also with no electricity. The mayor's team was obviously punishing us for not asking for the initial interrogator's office, which was the best office in the facility.

The two teams were both very upset because they had to undo everything they had done and reroute the computers once again, pack all the equipment once more and move it all to the new trailer. More upsetting was the fact that the new trailer had no air conditioning or electricity, and it had been hit by a mortar round during the week, leaving it full of holes. The Commander told us to move into it and that the mayor's team would have it fixed within the week, but he also added one more team to move into the trailer with us.

I went to look at the trailer and saw that the mortar round had shredded all of the upper right side. The left side had five big holes in the back that were so large I could see right through them. Furthermore, the trailer was in the center of the rocket attacks field, so the three teams' morale was totally shot to the curb. There was no doubt that the trailer would be hit again in the future: it was just a matter of time. I felt their problems weighing down on me. It is not easy for any interrogator to perform his work without a place to type reports. The three teams were tired from all the moving, packing and unpacking, disconnecting and reinstalling equipment every three days. But this was not the end. Reality had more surprises in store for us, and all of our troubles were the result of the attitudes of the two junior officers and their behavior toward each other.

Around the beginning of the third week, I was heavy into reporting. My draft book was full of reports every day, which I typed in the company's Command Office. It was all such an inconvenience: too many people were moving around, making the work impractical. I had to improvise and come up with an idea. I gave up on the notion that the person in charge of our groups was capable of providing us with what we needed; I faced reality and came to the conclusion that I had to do something. I could not jeopardize the troops' safety for more than two weeks, wondering when we would have an office. Therefore, I took initiative. Attacks on the base were increasing daily, Katusha rockets were shaking the ground every other day, and mortar rounds were hitting us when the rockets were not. I had to take immediate action because the pace of the command was too slow to provide us with adequate working conditions.

The Military Police (MP) provided physical security around the base, guarding all the gates, and I had a very good relationship with them because I had helped them with Arabic translation numerous times over the past few weeks. The East gate MPs had a break room which was sometimes empty, and there was a little storage space between the break room and an inspection room. I asked the person in charge to let me use this room to meet my informants. He said I could use it if I could pile all the boxes of food (MRE's) to one side. I did so and made a space of about 3 x 3 yards. Finally, I had my own place! I was not picky. The person in charge helped me move everything and even told me that he and his crew appreciated me and my team for keeping the troops safe. He told me that his troops would be fine, that losing the space was a matter of convenience they would sacrifice for their own safety. I thanked him and his generous troops.

The space was too small to fit seven troops in at one time,

so I divided the team in two. Three people could sit with me when I was talking to an informant. To ease the boredom and break the tension that had been building up over the past few weeks, I assigned a person to write the draft report while I was questioning an informant. I told the other two to watch. All the team members were happy, and the next day, I took another group of four to do the same. My team members were finally starting to relax.

They noticed the willingness of some Iraqis to cooperate. Not all of the Iraqis hated us. Some of my team members even asked me to assign a particular informant to them.

The team's morale was building again when we were hit with another reality check. All of my team members were suddenly reassigned to a mission in southern Iraq due to a shortage of interrogators in Hillah in Southeast Baghdad, an area dominated by Shiite Muslims. The area needed Persian speakers and translators, but this was not the case for interrogators, because some translators were provided. As an Arabic speaker and interrogator, I was to remain behind. My team members were in shock: Some of them were clapping their hands and others just stood there smiling, but wondering what was going on. I knew the feeling. They had just started their reports, only to be pulled to another area of Iraq. I thought, "Here I go again. I have no team."

So my former team and the other two teams had to pack again. We unplugged every computer and the other devices that had just been installed. We lost the doomed trailer, which was hit by a rocket two weeks later. God was merciful in that none of us were in it; we were prevented from devastation by the move. The base mayor never again assigned anyone to the trailer during the rest of my time on that base.

I was given another team and moved to another trailer for one week. Again, I lost this new team due to another shortage of intelligence personnel in Balad.

I was given yet another trailer with a team of four civilian contractors working for the Department of Defense. I soon lost one of them; in two more months the other lost me when I was attached to the U.S. Marine expeditionary units.

The last trailer was good. It had air conditioning and computers and it was not too far from the dining facility. Finally, I felt happy again. It took a full month and one week to find an office! Of course, my happiness did not last long. Reality struck again, and this time, it struck hard, shaking to the core the morale of most of the interrogators and intelligence agents. There was an unexpected change in the computer programming which made all but a few of the intelligence personnel stop reporting. We were trained in a system specifically made for intelligence, but in Iraq, there was a system designed by a civilian contractor that was totally different from our own. The civilian contractors refused to service our system because the change of command refused to let their server access it. Civilian contractors legally have no rights to access intelligence business, so the civilian contractors refused to serve our system. We were forced to work under the civilian contractors' operating system, which most of us were not familiar with. The new system was horrible; it was impractical to use with our work. Most of the intelligence personnel got discouraged and simply stopped reporting, blaming the system. We had to save what we were typing every ten minutes, or else we would lose the whole report. Our reports were not short — they required two to three hours of typing, so if we got carried away and forgot to save, we would lose everything. I understood why most of my colleagues stopped reporting.

I found myself working alone again. The safety and security of the troops was assigned to my team, a responsibility which I lost within a few days as they were deployed to Balad. I was given an armored vehicle to drive alone, which was an exception to the rules. You were supposed to drive with a buddy for safety. I had to drive alone to meet my contacts, making my job more difficult and stressful. It was hard. I had never before realized what a difference it made having just one other person around me. Only one Warrant Officer stood tall next to me, Warrant Officer Duffy (not his real name).

I was able to carry out the work of three intelligence team members, but there were challenges. I hate typing most of all, and Warrant Officer Duffy knew that, so he teamed up with me. We made up for the three teams we had lost to Tikrit, Kut, and Daywanyah. The well-being of the troops relied upon the work of Warrant Officer Duffy and me. We would stay up reporting until midnight, only to wake up at 6 A.M. and start all over again.

Chief Warrant Officer Duffy helped me to do excellent reports on time, and he was able to transmit them to theater command on time as well. We did miracles. We could have gotten Abu Mussab al Zarqawi, but technicalities stood in our way. On April 13, both of us were angry because my source had told me that he had been sitting next to Zarqawi in a mosque in Siggariah for two hours, but he had no telephone. I asked for a commercial phone for the local informant, but the answer was "negative." I asked for another commercial phone for the intelligence personnel to use with the local informants, but again, the answer was "negative." The Warrant Officer and I were so angry that every person noticed. We had worked so hard to catch Zarqawi, but our efforts were thwarted by something as simple as a telephone worth less than fifty dollars.

The next morning, Central Command finally okayed the telephone, but it was too little too late to catch Zarqawi once and for all.

We finally caught up with Zarqawi three weeks before my return. I found him posing as a tribal leader. He had an office in Baghdad next to the main hospital. He went underground again, and soon his groups killed four civilian contractors, hanged them and buried them on the street. It was on the news. One of my friends gave me the pictures.

Zarqawi had started aggressively attacking the supply lines between Jordan and Baghdad and between Kuwait and Hillah. Saudi and Baghdad paid the locals to attack it. Zarqawi had also paid $20,000 to kill a Marine striker, $10,000 to hit a HMMWV, and $5,000 to kill a translator or an Iraqi civilian that worked with multinational forces. By May of 2004, we had lost twenty seven Iraqi translators and civilian workers in Camp Victory, the Baghdad International Airport, and the Green Zone.

Three weeks after the Warrant Officer and I reported the mosque and Zarqawi's hiding place, an attack was conducted by the multinational task force. Zarqawi was in Syria as my informant had told me, but one of his lieutenants was captured in the same house. I was angered again because the raid was not good enough — it was too late, the action was based upon old intelligence I had reported a month ago, and Zarqawi did not stay in the same place for more than a day or two. He would leave and come back a week later in order to avoid being captured. We told them that, but it didn't help.

3

SPRINTING:

MID-MARCH TO END OF MAY, 2004

By the end of March 2004, I had a full understanding of the magnitude of the events going on around me. I understood that we were in real trouble. No accounts for Iraqi Army weapons. No accounts for Weapons of Mass Destruction. Our "fast and swift victory" created a lot of problems: in only twenty one days, we took all of Iraq, but where were the Iraqi Army's troops? Where were their weapons? Did our Army secure them? Destroy them?

I needed to find the answer. What I discovered shocked me and my commanding officers.

Iraqi Army weapons were hidden in schools, hospitals, and special underground bunkers all over the country. When the command acted on my report, and the prospective time maneuvering units moved to check the areas mentioned in my report, they found nothing. All of the weapons were stolen. My report was one year late because I had been deployed one year after the war began.

All the weapons — every single piece — was stolen and hidden from the Americans' reach. Some of the weapons were hidden in farms, berms, in irrigation canals and in the country-side. I visualized that not only the weapons were out there, but even more complicated issues.

The Sunnis who were Saddam's best friends, started aiding our bitter enemy, Zarqawi. I also visualized that we were too slow reacting to the events because the volume of them was too high. All the maneuvering units were overwhelmed by information that I had provided for them in just two months. I had identified more than a dozen groups that attacked us by mortars, set road bombs and Improvised Explosive Devices (IED's). Very little had been done about that. I recognized that we had a serious problem with reaction to these events.

Most of the weapons used on us were Russian or Belgian; short range mortars (60mm, 82mm, 120mm, 125mm) or Katusha rockets, Strella with maximum range of six miles or less. It would have been so easy to catch the attackers, but the maneuvering units' reaction procedures were too slow. I felt frustrated. I started to feel helpless because, most of the time, immediately after any mortar fire or rocket attack, one of my sources would come running to tell me who attacked us and from what location. I would rush to place my report with a special code on it for immediate reaction. My command was very cooperative — they always immediately forwarded the report to the theatre commander — but that is where the prob-lems would start.

The report fell under the theatre commander's priorities. Most of the time, the approval took a day or two. By then, it was too late.

I was struck by the harsh reality of the situation. I thought my reports would have been approved within minutes, but in reality, the mechanism of the reports goes like this: I would submit my report to the company command, then it would be transmitted to the battalion command, the brigade command, and then finally to the theatre command. After the theatre command had approved it, it would come back in the same sequence to my company command, then to the maneuvering unit to deploy the troops to find the attackers. By the time this process was over, Zarqawi's boys were long gone. Not only that, they were probably laughing at us. One day after another, attack after attack, we never reacted in time. Slowly, all the thugs who were attacking us realized that our reaction time was too slow, and the attacks began to increase.

Interrogators almost stopped reporting. Some maneuvering units refused to react to the theatre command's approval because they needed another two or three reports to support the first. Other maneuvering units said they did not have a sufficient number of troops to carry out the mission.

The attacks continued. Zarqawi's groups intimidated the civilian Iraqis who had witnessed their attacks on us. Sometimes, they would just shoot the civilians dead. Our sources were afraid of Zarqawi: He paid $5,000 to have a source killed, while we were not paying the sources *any* money. Sources were highly motivated Iraqis who volunteered their time, put their lives in danger, and sometimes even sacrificed their lives for us. They would come to see me on foot, running from house to house, building to building and hiding from others so they couldn't be identified. When a source saw me, it was as if he saw victory and success, as if he were seeing the best thing possible in his life. I felt so sad. I felt helpless. It was not my call to shoot back with the biggest gun. It was sad to see loving, brave men, who visualized and understood the meaning of freedom, standing in front of me, sweating and breathing heavily from running to deliver the most accurate information as quickly as they could, while the maneuvering units could not do anything without an order. I was disappointed in our mechanism.

I always gave each source a soda to drink and a hero story to keep him motivated. I told my source we had good reasons for not shooting back the way he had expected. It was so painful to me. I saw how disappointed my sources were in us. I saw my sources' generosity and acceptance . . . it is a hard feeling to describe.

April 11, 2003 was a day of anger for me. My story had reached the theatre's commanding general, and he sent a liaison to see me. I was angry because I had sent an urgent report concerning a plan that was carefully placed by the insurgents to carry out a large scale attack on multinational forces. The attack was planned to begin from Seven Nissan, a city in North Baghdad, to Taji City, formerly Saddam's Air Force Base. The attack was to proceed to the Green Zone in Baghdad through Abu Ghraib to Baghdad International Airport and Camp Victory main. The attack would be carried out on Arbainyah (Arbaiynah is the fortieth day after the death of the highest Shiite clerk, Ali).

The highest Shiite clerk Ali is the first cousin of the prophet Mohammed, the prophet of the Muslim people of the Islamic religion. A person who believes in Islam is a Muslim, not an Islamist as the media characterizes most of the time.

Shiites are people who believe in the Emam Ali way of Islam. There are three other ways of practicing Islam: the Maliki way of worship, which is the most moderate of the Muslim forms of worship; Hambally and Hanafi, which are also more moderate than Emam Ali, the Shiite way of worship.

The word Shiia itself means "party." The word Shiite means the person who worships as Emam Ali, Mohammed's cousin, does. So "Shiites" refers to the party of Emam Ali. The Shiite party is the dominant party in the religions of Iraq and Iran. In Iran, the Shiite party is known as the Bader party, and it is more political than religious. Presently, it is the most aggressive religious party in Iraq. Therefore, the Shiite party has made the anniversary of Emam Ali's death a religious celebration, which is not accepted by all Muslims other than the Shiites. Since Emam Ali's death has become a major religious event, the attack was ordered to be carried out in the early morning of the Arbainyah.

My source came running to me at 6 A.M. to tell me this. I was asleep when the East gate called my cell phone. I was really tired because I had gone to sleep at 1 A.M. The MP called me again, and I was half asleep when I answered. He told me that my source was there to speak with me, and that it was extremely urgent. I asked the MP to let him in the room and give him coffee and told the MP I would be with him in five minutes. I knew it must have been important because my source had told me the previous day that he would not come the next day. I dressed in two minutes and ran to the HMMWV, and three minutes later I was at the gate. I shook hands with the MP, who was my friend, filled my mug with coffee and entered the room to see Ms. Pago.

I knew instantly that she was serious. Her facial expression was different, and her demeanor announced the magnitude of what she was about to tell me. I met with Ms. Pago for three hours, ignoring my breakfast. It was almost lunch time before she finished drawing the map of the operation. Her story caught me by surprise, and I gave her extra attention. Two days were left before a major attack on us by the Mahadi Army. The Sunni Communists, combined with Saddam's sympathizers and former Bathists, were also in the party. Communists and Sunnis allied with their enemy, the Shiites, to attack us on a large scale.

Al Mahadi's Army was an armed militia that belonged to Moqtada Sader, who is presently the highest ranking Shiite clerk. Moqtada is the only son of Mohammed al Sader, the great-great grandson of the prophet Mohammed. However, King Hussein of Jordan is also a descendent of the prophet Mohammed.

Moqtada was six years old when his father was assassinated by the former Iraqi dictator Saddam Hussein. Mohammed al Sader was traveling in his vehicle with his wife and children when Saddam Hussein's secret police blocked his way and shot him and his family to death. Moqtada was in school that day; therefore, he was spared. He was raised an orphan by his relatives and his godfather, Emam Sistani.

Emam Sistani is living today and still acts as godfather to Moqtada. He is also the head of his own party, the Al Tayar Al Sadri party. This is the original party of Mohammed al Sader, Moqtada's father.

The Shiite party, which is headed by Moqtada and Al Tayar Al Sadri, has the same goals and principles, with only a few distinctions. One is that the Mahadi's Army belongs to Moqtada's Shiite party.

Al Tayar Al Sadri is the old way of Shiite worshipping, and it is most likely not involved in the political arena. Al Mahadi's Army had always protected the Shiite party and Al Tayar Al Sadri.

The Emam Ali Arbaynyah was only two days away. I was worried to death about the real obstacle though: the order mechanism. I thanked Ms. Pago, bought lunch for both of us, shook hands and said goodbye.

Shiites were the major players in the attack. They planned ahead of the Arbaiyniyah. They planted their troops in all the multinational bases and fobs. Most of the local Iraqi workers in the companies that operated in the bases were manned by Mahadi Army troops passing as casual workers. Most of the delivery trucks were Mahadi Army trucks. They planned to sneak the explosives in the sand and gravel trucks and park the trucks near the central command offices and residences. The mortar attack on Camp Victory main and Black Jack would begin at night before the morning of the Arbainyah; in the morning, suicide bombers would attack us in the dining facilities, the PX and the commissaries.

One day had passed since I submitted the report. No

decision was made. I left the company formation and drove the HMMWV to my quarters. I was really angry. I left my quarters to meet another source at the East gate. This source did not know the full details of the attack as Ms. Pago did, but she knew that one of his friends would participate in the attack on the Green Zone on Al Arbainyah day.

I went back and wrote a long report and sat in the company office until 2 A.M., asking the guys on duty if there was any response from the theatre command. The answer was no. Finally, I went to sleep. I strongly believed my informant: she had never lied to me. She never came back to ask what happened this time. I tossed and turned in my bed until 4 A.M. before I went to sleep.

I woke up at 6 A.M. and went to the dining facility to eat breakfast, then went to company formation. I left for the East gate to wait for one of my sources who was scheduled to see me at 8 A.M.

My source came on time. I gave him a cup of coffee and we started talking about our subject. My source was busy talking and I was busy writing when somebody knocked on my door. I opened the door halfway to prevent my source from being seen. It was my friend, the MP, and he told me I was needed in the company office. I asked him, "Why? Who needs me?" but he told me that he did not know. I asked him to take care of my source, and to make sure that no one saw him.

I rushed to the company office and I found the commander waiting for me at the door. I knew it must be an important matter. The Commander told me that the theatre commanding general wanted to know whether or not the attack was for real.

I told the Commander to tell the general to wait ten more hours and see for himself. The commander laughed. He told me that an Australian warrant officer was inside waiting to see me because the general had sent him to talk to me.

I entered the room and saw a young man in his early twenties sitting in a chair. He had on a khaki uniform, but it was a different design from mine and everyone else's in the room. He had on a bullet-proof vest, and his pistol was on the left side of his belt. His shining eyes reflected his intelligence and his smile indicated his politeness. Immediately, he stood up and started walking toward me and the commander. The commander introduced us, and I shook hands with him and sat down. The general told the chief to ask me whether or not I trusted the source. The chief told me that the general wanted to know if there were any other people who had a report about the attack.

I told the chief that I trusted the source because my source's brother was one of the people participating in the attack. My source's brother urged my source to let us know. My source had told me this a day and a half ago. I told the chief that the answer to his second question was negative: no other person had reported on this matter other than me.

The Australian looked at me and asked, "We don't have much time, do we?" I told him to tell his boss that, because I had known for nearly two days.

The chief left the company to go to the central command building and tell the general. I left the company to go to the East gate to continue my meeting with my source.

The general ordered that the base be closed immediately. The Green Zone was also closed and all the workers were expelled. They banned all the workers' trucks and delivery trucks from entering any multinational base until one day after the Arbainyah. The general's decision was indescribable: it was quick and effective.

The attack was carried out by the insurgents on time, but they got a big surprise: their attack was completely phased out. They were only able to destroy one tank and one HMMWV at the Shula Bridge.

The insurgents' boldness to attack us under Zarqawi encouraged Moqtada Sader, the Shiite religious leader. Two months after the attempt, we had a larger insurgency in the three largest cities in the Southeast of Baghdad: Najaf, Karbala and Fallujah. Najaf and Karbala are the holiest Shiite cities and the site of the shrine of Emma Ali, the cousin of the prophet Mohammed, who is buried in one of them. The two holy princes Hassan and Al Hussein are buried in Karbala. All three cities were full of all kinds of arms, and these arms were in the hands of very angry people who did not like us very much.

Mortar attacks, road bombs and improvised explosive devices increased, and my sources decreased.

Then disaster struck that made Iraq what it is now. In May of 2004, Mr. Paul Brimmed ordered the release of all Iraqi prisoners.

Paul Brimmed was a civilian appointed by the Bush administration to govern Iraq before the transitional Iraqi government. He destroyed our victory. It was a fatal mistake. I believe Mr. Brimmed thought that releasing all the Iraqi prisoners would make the Iraqi people happy. I believe that he thought that the transition of the government to the Iraqis in June would be easier if he released the prisoners in May, but it was the worst decision that had ever been made about Iraq. Vicious killers — people who had beheaded others, murderers and rapists — were now free.

By May of 2004, Iraq had been liberated for about a year and a half. Many problems were already on our hands. There was a lack of jobs, and a lack of food and water. There was no electricity. There was no Iraqi legal system, no Iraqi police, and no Iraqi army. All of these factors combined and some of the former Iraqi government officials had stopped working without pay; others had stolen what they could get their hands on and left Iraq. Suddenly, Mr. Brimmer released cut-throat criminals into the public streets. Mr. Brimmer had killed us all and set back the situation by letting out every prisoner in the entire Iraqui prison system. What a genius!

The last two weeks of May 2004, the mortar attacks on bases and road IEDs were heavy in volume until the command ordered the seizure of the missions of the base after 5 P.M.

On June 1, 2004 the Iraqi transitional government took over Iraq. To our surprise, everything came to a stop for over two weeks. Ayyad Allawi and Abdul-Aziz al Hakim took over the new Iraq. Most of us do not know why the shooting at bases stopped. IED's also slowed noticeably. Personally, I thought that the Iraqis and al Zarqawi were afraid of the new Iraqi government. I thought they were having flashbacks, fearing that the new government might find them and prosecute them. They were testing the situation.

The honeymoon did not last long. Sader did not like the

new government, and he felt that Iraq was slipping away from him. Immediately, he started to attack the new government by using his army. The Iraqis who were unemployed and hungry joined the Sader army. The huge number of cut-throat killers that Mr. Brimmed released had gone after the big bucks — they joined Zarqawi's army and made a nice name for themselves: "the Mujahedeen." Zarqawi paid them $30,000 to kill a single Marine striker, $20,000 to destroy a supply truck, and $10,000 to destroy a HMMWV; $10,000 to kill a translator and $5,000 to attack any multinational base or FOB (Smaller Army Base) by mortars.

Iraq became hell on earth in 2004. Bombs were everywhere. Mortars and shots rang, rockets whizzed over our heads every day.

Zarqawi dominated the West of Iraq one hundred percent. Our supply lines were devastated under his constant attacks. The Army had changed the convoy supply route, but Zarqawi had followed the supply line. We lost hundreds of eighteen wheelers and hundreds of foreign civilian drivers, along with hundreds of U.S. troops that had escorted the convoys.

Zarqawi himself had gone underground. He was well liked and admired by Iraqis in the West. My source also disappeared. I tried to find him, but no one knew where he was. I am afraid to tell his full name because I do not want to expose him.

On May 14, 2004 my source, Mr. Digman, came to see me at midday. He was very dirty and his pants and shirt were muddy, as if he had rolled in a wet pit full of mud. His pant legs were torn from both knees down; his shirtsleeves were torn from the elbows down, too. His hair was full of mud, and it was not combed. His face was unshaven, and his fingernails were dirty. Even his shoes were dirty with mud. Needless to say, he smelled bad. After all, he was also really tired. I asked him where he had been, and he told me that he had been arrested in Fallujah with a lot of other people, and the Iraqi police had released him that day. When I asked him why he was arrested, he told me that there was a raid on his neighborhood and he was arrested with everyone else. I told him that I was unable to ask anyone about him because I did not want to reveal his identity. He told me that no one in that area knew him. I gave him my lunch and my Coca-Cola, and he ate as if he had not eaten in days. He asked for a cigarette, so I borrowed one from the MP and gave it to him. He told me that he wanted to go see his mother in Ramadi, a city in Northeast Baghdad. He finished smoking and stood up to leave. I walked him out of the room, and he gave me a very long hug and said goodbye. He hugged me as though he would never see me again. I felt that he didn't want me to know what was going on in his life, but I wished that he had. I never saw him again. I can only hope that he is out there somewhere, alive. I hope to see him again, to thank him for what he did for us.

4

THE FALLUJAH WAR:
JUNE, 2004

Things were getting worse every day. The U.S. Marines decided to go to war with the Mahady Army and Zarqawi in the West at the same time. They were tired of the Mahady and Zarqawi running wild. The Marines submitted their request to the theatre command to furnish them with highly trained and capable teams of interrogators. They asked to get natives, if possible. I understood that the Marines were going to fight religious fanatics in Fallujah: Muslim fighters are both fierce and brave, and they strongly believe they will go to paradise when they die, so native interrogators were important in this situation.

I was selected to support the Marines. The three cities they targeted were dominated by Shiites, and the Sunnis, Saddam's accomplices and Zarqawi were ready to support the Shiites fight against us. The war was between Fallujah, Hillah and

Baghdad, and the terrain was not good for a ground fight because the dirt roads were narrow and the area had rivers and irrigation canals. The Iraqis' nicknamed the place the Death Triangle, and my team and I were dispatched to the center of it, stationed between the worst cities: Exandaryah, Mahmodyah and Lalifyah (which the locals also referred to as Al Musayb.

The three cities fall in a flat land, a semi-delta stretched between the Euphrates and Tigres in South Baghdad. The landscape is distinguished by its high number of irrigation canals — there are thousands of them. Narrow roads, high date palms, and hundreds of thousands of sugar cane strips grew by the irrigation canals, separating the green fields and the corn fields from each other.

Navigating the roads was impossible. We got doused in mud and clay faster than you could imagine. We were lucky if the vehicle didn't flip over. The terrain was completely dangerous, but this was not disastrous to us; on the contrary, it was a disaster to the insurgency. Unfortunately, they knew that.

Musayb was home to the only broadcasting station, the one where the Minister of Information told his infamous lie, "There are no Americans in Iraq. The nearest Americans are at the border of Kuwait." We had already taken down Saddam's statues in Baghdad and occupied the Baghdad International Airport.

The broadcasting station was demolished by the Marines and they built a base on it. This was the worst possible place for it because the former broadcasting station was in the middle of Saddam's most favored tribes: Dolaymi, Al Jaboory and Al Himayri. The Jabor tribe stretched from Baghdad to the South of Exanderyah city in Musyab area. Himairi stretched from Exanderyah to Hillah, South of Baghdad. The Dolaymi tribe stretched from South Baghdad, west of both the Jabor tribe and the Himairi tribe towards Dayarah and Jibalah cities, southwest of Baghdad. Most of them were Sunnis and were very angry over losing Saddam, and yet the Marines had built their base in the middle of them. Good God.

I found myself in the middle of all this, acting as one of the major players that everyone counted on. The base was designated to be the primary detention facility and interrogation post. From there, prisoners were dispatched to Abu Ghraib and other detention facilities. I was heavily occupied as the number of prisoners increased each day. My lack of sleep became noticeable. Fatigue and loss of appetite took its toll on me and the others. Every one of us had done more than our normal capabilities. I felt most comfortable separating myself from the rest of them in order to start targeting the local tribe surrounding us. Some of my team members and Marine Hit Teams carried out the interrogation process.

On June 15, 2004 I started looking for local sources. Finding sources that belong to a tribe who loves Saddam was a great challenge. The war was on, and it was fierce. Many of the casualties were young Marines. I had to act fast to find sources to lead me to where the Shiites were getting their weapons and supplies. I needed to know the best routes taken by the Shiites and Zarqawi and their fighting schedules. I had to feed intelligence to the theatre command.

I jumped in my HMMWV and started driving around the

area surrounding the base hunting for sources. It didn't take too long to find a few good ones because there were still many people around the Death Triangle who hated Saddam. I started pouring intelligence reports to the theatre command: three weeks later, the Marines took Fallujah down along with Najaf and Hillah. What led to the quick victory was actually something unexpected.

From London, Ayatollah Sustani ordered Mogtada al Sader to stop fighting the Americans and join the politics or he would suspend his religious title. Ayatollah Sustani is Mogtada al Sader's godfather, so he stopped, and the Marines won the war. The short honeymoon between the Sunnis, Shiites, Zarqawi and Saddam's sympathizers was over.

All of Mahadi's Army stopped fighting us except one group,the Al Hussein Flag, who later called themselves the Al Hussein Brigade's special group. Later on, this group became a nightmare for us.

U.S. Marines had secured the three supply routes from Saudi to Baghdad, Kuwait to Baghdad and Jordan to Baghdad. We were happy. The defeated Sunnis had retreated Northwest of Baghdad to Khanzdri City, Abu Ghraib City, and Taji City areas. Zarqawi had gone farther, to Ramadi City in Northeast Baghdad; to Baqubah City in Northwest Baghdad; and to the North, around Ramadi and Baqubah. Al Hussein's special groups hid themselves in the area between Hillah Fallujah and Jarf al Sakkar — next to where the Marines were stationed, in Mussayb. The special groups soon made Exandaryah, Mahmodyan, Latifyah and Mussayb a living hell.

5

ONGOING PROBLEMS:
JUNE, 2004

Iraqi Communists are Sunnis who had served Saddam's Bathist party over the past thirty five years. They are more oriented to power than their rival Shiites, who mostly depended on their vast majority in Iraq. The Communists decided to throw all the tricks in the book in our faces. They licked their wounds from the war in Fallujah, regrouped and reorganized, then decided to take over the new Iraqi Army. They flooded recruiting centers and came prepared. Most of them knew that we would not recruit them if we knew they were former Bathists; therefore, the Communists exploited the recruiting centers by using Bathist party ugliness. All the hard-core Communists went to the recruiting agents with sad stories about what the former Bathist party had done to them or their family members. Some of them would stop in the middle of questioning, interrupting their stories to stand and pull up their shirts and show old wounds or scars inflicted on them by Saddam's Bath party. In all honesty, those scars and wounds could have been inflicted by us during the war. They fooled both the screeners and the recruiters, and group after group of these Communists joined the new Iraqi Army. They brought civilians with them, friends and family members from their neighborhoods.

The pay was good, better than what most Iraqis made. They bought cars and land and were still able to save some money.

We unintentionally helped the communists to take over the new Iraqi Army. We didn't know their tricks.

The Army units that formed in different areas to protect the citizens became responsible for scaring these people. Members of the Army and police units took over the small businesses in their areas, providing workers from their own tribes to American companies and foreign companies working on multinational bases. They also hijacked local contracts with us to provide things like ice, fresh meat, and even custodians.

The Communists' plans did not stop. They knew that Mr. Brimmer's thugs, killers and rapists were out and needed jobs. They knew that Al Hussein's brigade was made up of these kinds of criminals. The Communists started to harass the Iraqis who worked with Americans in an attempt to set Al Hussein's brigade's special groups on the Iraqis who supported us on all the bases. The special groups were always around the bases in the past, but they never dared to touch a worker until they were set up by these cunning, former Bathists.

It was a disaster. The harassment became a legal, Islamic jihad on every Iraqi person who worked on the American bases. Al Hussein's special groups began legally killing Iraqi civilian workers. Religious leaders agreed about the killing of people who helped the occupants: they declared that every person working with multinational forces would be treated as an enemy of Iraq.

They were not able to fight us with weapons, but they were able to stop local workers from working with us.

6

AL HUSSEIN'S BRIGADE SPECIAL GROUPS

The special groups turned out to be bigger than anyone expected. Their presence around multinational bases intimidated the workers greatly, and the special groups were given sympathy by religious clerks.

The special groups moved in for the kill. Most of the multinational civilian companies were located on the bases, along with most of the local Iraqi civilian companies. These multinational bases are the centers of money; the special groups began presenting threatening letters to local employers on the bases, telling them to abandon their work or they would be killed. These letters were placed on the doors of employees' homes and cars or even given to them by hand. The terrified employees would run to their companies with these letters seeking some form of protection; these companies then looked to us for help.

I was dispatched to investigate. I met with executives from the base's companies and the employees who had been threatened. I saw the fear in their eyes, and the worry in the faces of the executives.

I wrote report after report through the chain of command. I explained the depth of the problem and the fear among these people. Soon my chain of command responded with their bitter answer: we could not become involved in any domestic problems including the protection of Iraqi civilians. I was told to tell the executives from foreign and local companies to protect their own employees. The decision was a disaster.

The problem was delivering the message to the angry executives of these companies and their fearful employees. I recalled a book I had read in college, *Flock Catcher* by Shelby Steel. A flock catcher is a person who meets with an angry crowd to diffuse a sensitive situation. Sometimes the crowd is not angry, but has serious questions that require careful answers. The Speaker of the House in Congress is a good example of a flock catcher; when journalists swarm Congress asking questions about sensitive political situations, especially those having to do with the decisions of the President of the United States, the flock catcher fields them. It gets difficult, however, when the flock expects positive answers.

Flock catchers have excellent capabilities for improvisation and almost supernatural common sense that guides them through difficult situations created by their superiors.

The thugs from the special groups heard about the decision. They knew we could not protect the locals outside the base's parameters.

The next day, three girls who worked at the Baghdad International Airport were killed. One was cut in half with a sword. One was shot thirty times in the chest. The last girl was shot in the head.

The worst thing was that our reasoning to excuse the problem ended up dumping it on the Iraqi local authorities.

Zahra, one of the girls who were cut in half, was an orphan. She was raised by her brother and her uncle after her father was killed in the war between Iran and Iraq. She was an excellent accountant, but had been out of a job for the past three years. She had just gotten a job with one of the dignitaries guard security companies at the base.

She spoke English well, which was hard to find in a communist country where most of the people who spoke foreign languages only knew Russian. Her personality was so great that she was loved by all those who worked with her. She even brought local food from her uncle's house to the American and Iraqi civilian workers at her job. She was a really loving, caring, and sweet human being whose life was wasted by a vicious, rotten criminal out there slaughtering people in the name of God.

I felt like my heart was bleeding from the pain caused by the memory of her smiling face. How could I tell her bosses that we were not obligated to protect her? Who exactly were we obligated to protect?

I wondered why we didn't create a law that enabled us to protect sweet Zahra and others who pioneered their love and commitment to us and to the future of their country, Iraq. Zahra had died in vain. She had died without the protection of her father, her job, or her country, and today we were giving her the cold shoulder because of obtuse legalities.

I understand how hard it is to be a flock catcher because I have a big heart that will never forgets sweet Zahra and the more than three hundred who were slaughtered after her.

I went to the East gate to find a huge crowd of Iraqi civilians waiting to ask me what the Americans were going to do about the murder of these three girls. I knew that we would do nothing. Our policy was clear: we could not get involved in Iraq's local problems. Outside the base, murder is under the jurisdiction of local authority.

I personally knew the three girls. I had talked to them several times before their deaths, and I admired their bravery and patriotism. Arab women do not often work outside the home, but the three of them were hard working accountants who were well-spoken. I was sad that I was not able to help them.

Threatening letters increased along with murders. The effect was becoming more frightening. Employees would leave their jobs after receiving their paychecks, and foreign and domestic companies experienced a shortage of labor. Most projects came to a stop, affecting schools, hospitals, local clinics and roads.

Many executives from the companies went to the war theatre command asking for some kind of help because the matter was out of control. Iraq's local authority was unable to do anything because there *was* no local authority. Period. The thugs from the special groups were armed and dangerous.

Again I was dispatched to talk to the executives and to find any solution possible. I wondered why I was charged with finding a solution: I was not Paul Brimmer, the man responsible for creating this mess, by letting the prisoners out of all the prisons in Iraq. Again, Shelby Steel's book came to mind, and I decided to call my source, the Sheik Armstrong.

He came the next day. I sat with him and we talked for a long time, thinking of possible solutions to the problem. Sheik Armstrong suggested many things, some of which were good, but some that were expensive, such as making checkpoints outside the perimeters of the bases, which was eventually done. Other suggestions were more reasonable; for example, he told me to involve sheiks from the local areas since the bases were built on their lands. He also suggested giving local contracts to the people from areas surrounding the bases.

I wrote my report and took it to the command. A few days later, I was requested to accompany some commanders from the Core of Engineers to speak with our area's sheik concerning hiring a local contractor to cut the grass around the base. I usually advised the companies to hire locals living around the bases to minimize movement so the workers would not have to travel long distances.

The sheik's ideas worked. Slowly, the workers returned. But the aggressiveness of the special groups attracted Zarqawi: he started hiring them to begin attacking supply lines again.

7

ZARQAWI'S
ADAPTABILITY

The aggressiveness of the special groups convinced Zarqawi to employ them. He had a lot of money, but no personnel. His willingness and commitment to fight us was greater than we knew. His plan was to recruit any Iraqi who was able to carry a weapon to join his group. He believed that the thugs in the special groups would be an excellent resource for attacking our supply routes.

Ahmed Abu Musab al Zarqawi and his lieutenant, Mr. Digman, along with two others, started to drive around the bases in armed, white, extended cab pick-up trucks recruiting the special groups, offering "Half Dafters" to the people who joined Zarqawi's group; this was the equivalent of $5,000 U.S. dollars! Ahmed knew that the special groups consisted of thieves and murderers like him. He knew that they would rub out our supply convoys for free. Ahmed offered the special groups money to gain their trust. Special groups decreased around base after base. Zarqawi took them to Al Anbar province and trained them to ambush the convoys. Zarqawi's tactics were simple, but deadly. They were swift and extremely successful. His success came from his natural knowledge of the area. He had grown up there. His tribe herded sheep and other animals between Jordan and Iraq.

His tactic was to place two to four road bombs in the specially chosen location. Then he would place two RPG (Rocket Propelled Grenade) men on the convoy site and place two PKC (Russian Long-range Machine Gun) men by the side of the road and provide two to three rifle men to support the RPG men. They would then detonate the IEDs, first on the escorted armed vehicles, and strike any undamaged armored vehicles with the RPG rockets. They would then open fire on the confused civilian convoy drivers. Three to five deadly minutes, and hell would freeze over. The rifle men would hunt the surviving civilians, sometimes burning everything, sometimes driving the supply trucks away to sell the goods in downtown Baghdad inside the East gate.

The East gate to Baghdad, *Al Bab al Shargi*, was in the Green Zone, an area partially open to the public. We liked to go to the Green Zone to eat Chinese food at a restaurant run by a Chinese-American. There was also fine local food at Iraqi restaurants in the Green Zone.

Soon after Al Zarqawi employed the thugs from the special groups to his group, American goods began surfacing in small quantities in *Al Bab al Sharqi*'s local markets. Digital cameras, televisions, radios, CDs, watches and other goods we could buy in the PX or Army commissary were available in the local markets. The prices were so low I had to laugh because the people selling our goods had no idea about the real value of the goods.

The fact was that these vendors were afraid of being arrested. They knew that everything in their possession was obtained illegally: the troops had paid for everything that the vendors had stolen. Soon, the *Al Bab al Sharqi* was flooded with American merchandise. The news spread to all the American troops in Baghdad, and later, to troops all over Iraq. You could buy a digital camera worth two or three hundred dollars in the U.S. for thirty-five dollars in the market; thumb drives that sold for eighty dollars in America were being sold for five dollars. Soon, GIs were going everywhere in *Al Bab al Sharqi*. The Iraqis selling our goods were happy with the prices we paid for the goods because they converted it to Iraq's currency: one American dollar equaled fifteen hundred Iraqi dinars, and one hundred dollars equaled 150,000 Iraqi dinars. Imagine making in one day what you made in one whole month under Saddam's rule! During that time, a month's pay was about 90,000 dinars, so these vendors were making a killing.

Even though the merchandise being sold was originally ours, and the people selling it killed our troops in convoys to get it, American GIs were happy to buy it.

However, the low prices didn't last too long because the number of Americans increased in *Al Bab al Sharqi*. The American GIs caused prices to double and eventually triple because of their smart comments about the low pricing. Nevertheless, the prices were still half of what was paid for the same item in the PX or the commissary.

Soon the news reached me. I was told that the prices at the market were good, and I was not too far from the Green Zone. The problem was that the path from my base to the Green Zone was a deadly one, full of IEDs and road bombs. Still, I decided to take the risk and check it out. It was not a good idea, but Rambo said that the truth was that we were expendable for the well-being of one another. I packed my team and hit the road. We went to the now infamous *Al Bab al Sharqi*. It was incredible! The East gate was a huge arched wall with a square wall surrounding it. A dome on the right side and a walled fence stretched from the left side of the arch wall. Right behind the arch gate there was a building on the right that seemed to be a recruiting center for one of the multinational forces' civilian companies. On the left side, another building stood which was also used as an office of some kind. We passed quickly through the gate without paying too much attention to screaming locals who were trying to be recruited into jobs as translators.

We passed a crowded restaurant and turned right onto a dirt road on the second block. Within two hundred yards we reached what looked like a swap meet (a flea market). It was set up right in the middle of the road; little booths were everywhere. About fifteen HMMWVs were parked before the colorful booths that lay side by side like jeweled necklaces on the ground. We parked our own six vehicles and swarmed our way through the crowd. It was full of American merchandise, and

GIs were everywhere. We found parking by a little dirt road and joined the crowd. It was truly unbelievable. The prices were so low they were nearly giving this merchandise away. Every member of my team bought something.

The reason the prices were so low was because the people selling did not really know what they were selling. They did not even know the names of the things they were selling because they didn't speak English very well. They only knew that the goods were American and that the American would buy them. The GIs were all over the merchandise like bees on honey.

You could buy digital cameras that sold for three hundred dollars in the U.S. for fifty dollars. They were selling flash disks and thumb drives for five dollars. Countless goods taken from our supply convoys were right there before our eyes, and everyone was happily filling his hands with whatever they would hold.

Suddenly, my defense mechanism kicked in: I vowed to catch the devil behind all of this. Zarqawii, whose groups were killing us, somehow managed to make us his customers! We were buying our own goods from him! I decided then and there to fight him. I needed to find a smart source to lead me to where the goods were coming from. I knew that Zarqawi and his top lieutenants from the special groups were behind this.

I went back to the base, made my plans, and returned to the Green Zone. I stopped in *Al Bab al Sharqi*, and while my team members spread out to buy what they wanted, I went looking for a source. My team members would distract me occasionally asking me to translate Arabic for them, so it took me over an hour to find a source. I gave him a nickname: Mr. East. I asked him to come see me there at the Baghdad International Airport, and he promised to be there in less than a week.

I returned to the base and told my friends who were MPs to let him see me if he came. I told them to find me no matter what, even if I was in a meeting with the highest commanding general. I must find Zarqawi.

Mr. East did come, and I rushed to meet him. I was so happy to see him because the theories I had read about in our books on finding sources really worked. That plus my unique style contributed to the success of finding this source.

Mr. East was very nervous. He did not want to stay. He told me that he only came because he had given me his word. He told me that the facilities and buildings and even some of the police worked with Zarqawi and the special groups. He told me that he was identified because one of the Facilities and Building Police (FB) guys saw him talking to the Americans. Mr. East told me that he could not come back again because he would be beheaded by Zarqawi personally. I gave him a Coca-Cola, and on his way out he suggested that I find a source from the FBs. It was a good idea. I never saw him again. The local market at *Al Bab al Sharqi* and the Green Zone cafes were bombed due to the presence of our troops.

Zarqawi was gaining confidence and experience to take us down with his war. He added a lot of Facilities and Building Police (FBs) to his collection of thugs. I nicknamed them the "black masked" men. The FB elements were armed police created by Saddam to guard government facilities and housing in all Iraqi cities. They were the most ideal elements to employ in order to create a war in the cities because they knew the cities better than most of the people who lived in them. At the same time, Ahmed's special groups were attacking convoys on supply routes at the freeways. He let the special groups join with the FBs elements in the city, creating disorder when there were so many convoys.

Zarqawi had a specific purpose in joining these two groups: intimidating the contractors, owners of local companies, and casual workers, who worked on bases. Zarqawi wanted to force them to compromise and feed him information about the supply convoys' schedules to know when they left their point of origin and arrived at their destinations. He started organizing times to kill in order to grab our attention.

One week in May of 2004, a minibus in Baghdad transporting nineteen janitors to the airport were stopped by Zarqawi's special groups in the middle of Seventeen November Bridge and executed in front of the public.

That same week, a contractor who had received $150,000 U.S. from our Core of Engineers was shot dead in his garage before he could use the money to pay his employees. The money had disappeared.

Also that same week, a local source was shot in the head in front of the main gate at the Baghdad International Airport.

This same style of killing through terror was carried out in every city in Iraq that had multinational bases. It was designed to intimidate and to cause panic.

Local contractors and workers compromised because we could not protect them. Zarqawi laid out his demands to them: he wanted to know the exact time of departure for each supply convoy, how many vehicles were in the convoy, and how many of the vehicles were armored. He demanded to know the makes and models of the vehicles in the convoy and the details of the goods they carried.

Workers and contractors who compromised were allowed to live. They sold us for their own survival.

The number of Zarqawi's groups increased, and he created small groups consisting of five men that he called "lines." The line is a section in the known army structure. The lines were armed with one RBG, one PKG and three AK-47s. Every ten lines worked under one finance officer who dispatched them when the area commander, or "*Amir*," needed them to attack a convoy. Zarqawi hired very important people in the Iraqi social structure called Mukhtars. These were people important during Saddam's time who worked together with FBs to secure law and order in the community. The Mukhtars never liked us.

Zarqawi ordered the Mukhtars to do what they did best: provide surveillance over our movements and report them to the finance officers. They reported the colors, makes and models of the vehicles we drove in their neighborhoods, how many wheels the vehicles had, and whether or not the vehicles had mounted weapons on them. They even reported the way the people driving the vehicles were dressed and the color of the patches on their uniforms, any weapons the soldiers carried, and the types and numbers of radios they used. We were watched closely by Zarqawi once the Mukhtars were on his payroll.

The Mukhtars became the first people to meet the patrol convoys in the neighborhoods they controlled.. They would stare at soldiers' shoulder patches as if they were rare diamonds. IEDs sprung up everywhere in the neighborhoods, and even though our routes changed from time to time, the IEDs always followed.

Zarqawi had done so well that Osama Bin Laden declared him a prince of Al Qaeda in Iraq. Bin Laden's support made Zarqawi very popular — thousands of young Iraqis joined his movement. His line numbers increased to remarkable numbers.

Zarqawi's ability to adapt to evolving situations helped him to stand in the fight. He changed his tactics again to add more members to his growing army. First, he organized his lines' activities into zones and sectors. Every finance officer was in charge of fifty lines in a particular zone and sector. The sectors were the equivalent of a country to Americans. They used their lines to plant road bombs in their portion of the supply routes and in the Mukhtars' neighborhoods to attack the convoys as well at the Amir's demands. Then he introduced a reward system for the attacks. Zarqawi's reward system was ingenious and it created devastating attacks on our multinational bases. He assigned a price to every action. Before being given the reward, a video had to be presented to support the actions because the prices were so high. Killing a Marine Striker was worth $20,000 U.S. dollars; killing two or three "infidels" in a HMMWV or planting IEDs on any multinational route paid $10,000 U.S. dollars; killing a local translator garnered $5,000 U.S. dollars, as did attacking any multinational base by one mortar round.

The reward system was so successful that a young Mustafas in Al Mahmudia destroyed nine convoys with five line members: Zarqawi declared him a prince and nicknamed him *Abu Sayaf*. Another line leader in Al Mahwed's judicial district destroyed nine convoys and took seven eighteen wheelers, a large generator and a caravan to his house.

Zarqawi's continuous success created a tribal criminal movement who called themselves the Islamic Army Mujahidin. Its only purpose was highway robbery. They created illegal checkpoints in their tribal areas to collect toll fees. Zarqawi's special groups' success in driving away eighteen wheelers loaded with free American goods was too good to be true, and the Islamic Army wanted their share of the pie. Since the Zarqawi lines of special groups were small minorities scattered around supply lines, the tribal criminals in the Jaish Al Islam were able to override them in their tribal territories.

Tribal members and tribal sheiks were of equal power in Saddam's time — the sheiks had no political or social weight under his reign. Jaish Al Islam knew that the sheiks in their tribal areas could not resist making a free dollar from Zarqawi's special groups. Jaish Al Islam was thieves stealing from the original thief, and tribal sheiks had fallen into the game. Jaish Al Islam became the legitimate tribal entity. They shared their toll fees with the tribal sheiks, and Zarqawi succeeded in spreading disorder to tribal areas. The toll fees spread over the entirety of Iraq's provinces.

Nevertheless, Zarqawi's movement upset a few good

sheiks who decided to help us and guide us in fighting Ahmed Abu Mussab. For example, Sheik Goodman stuck his neck out for our benefit when he came to see me.

8

ISLAMIC ARMY MUJAHIDIN "JAISH AL ISLAM":

JUNE, 2004-2006

Sheik Goodman wanted to prove a point. Sheik Goodman's anger sprung from Zarqawi's success in controlling Exandryah, Mahmudyah and Latifyah. Control of these three cities meant control of the Death Triangle.

Sheik Goodman was a former Iraqi Intelligence Coloncl. He was transferred to another branch before the liberation of Iraq. Zarqawi made the Death Triangle hell after he implemented the reward program. Sheik Goodman came to save us.

Sheik Goodman was about 5'11" and weighed around 280 pounds. He had grey hair and a round face with sharp, eagle eycs surrounded by black lashes. His small nose sat above a mustache which stretched to meet a neatly trimmed beard. He always dressed in the traditional clothing of an Arabian sheik, exactly like Omar Sharif in the film *Lawrence of Arabia*, and he would draw his gown around him in the same way whenever he walked toward me, slowly and with confidence. Sheik Goodman had the pleasant smile of a grandfather despite the two armed guards who always followed him with their eyes until he passed through security at the gate.

I was a little worried when I heard the news that a sheik at the Sand gate was asking to see me. I thought that he could be a suicide bomber. I asked the guard how the sheik knew about me, and the guard replied that he did not know. I told the guard to go back to talk to the sheik, to take him inside and search him. While he asked the sheik questions, I would be nearby, watching. I told the guard not to let the sheik know that I was the one parking near the gate; the guard did so, and he told me when the sheik was cleared.

I went to greet the Sheik and took him to my meeting place, where I gave him a Pepsi. The Sheik told me about himself, about the people of Iraq and their psychology.

"Listen to me carefully," he said. "I am your true friend. I am very wealthy. I do not want a reward from you or your government. I am here to help you. I am here to tell you the truth about how the Iraqis view your country, America. The truth is going to hurt you, but I am your friend, and a friend is the one who tells you the truth that no one dares to tell you."

Again, he asked me to listen carefully. I assured him that I was all ears. I also assured him that the truth would never make me angry. I asked him to continue.

Iraqis believed that Zarqawi was winning the fight with the Americans. Zarqawi came back after the war in Fallujah very determined and very strong. He said we must fight like Bedouin — we must fight Zarqawi the way that *he* fights. "Tell your general to close the roads and exits in Zarqawi's face, there are three main routes Zarqawi uses to move his groups to the Sunni area in Baccubah and the Diyalah province."

The Al Fallujah Ramadi Baccubah was a bad freeway for Zarqawi because it was well guarded by the Americans. The Sheik went on to say that Zarqawi was not stupid enough to use that freeway, and that Zarqawi would not use the Al Fallujah Baghdad freeway for the same reason. He said the best route for Zarqawi was the semi-street that went from Fallujah through Jarf al Sakar to Exandryah, Sowayrah, Jibbalah, Salman Pack to Baccubah; then, from the Baccubah Diyalah Bridge to an exit heading toward the northern cities.

Sheik Goodman told me to close the Jarf al Sakkar road that went from Fallujah to Sawayrah and Jibbalah — it was easy to close since it crossed the Presidential Canal, which had one main bridge and four small bridges. Sheik Goodman instructed me to close all five bridges because it would lock Zarqawi outside of the Death Triangle.

He said there would be four other indigenous tribes: Jabur, Dolaym, Humair and Al Janabi. Even though the four tribes were not all Sunni, they liked Saddam. Sheik Goodman insisted that I establish a good rapport with them by going off base and interacting with the people. He told me that I had created good feelings toward the Americans among the people in the area, which was why he came to help. Sheik

Goodman said that he loved America and the American people and that he wished all Iraqis understood what freedom meant, regardless of how it occurred.

He also told me to go out and see the children in schools, to give them candy and school supplies. He assured me that they would like me. He also advised me to go to local hospitals and to the market; he said that I would not be killed because I was already liked and respected. He said that the people already had a good attitude toward me because of how I treated the people in the interrogation room. Sheik Goodman then gave me a comprehensive map to show me what I should do to phase Zarqawi out of the Death Triangle.

I wrote my report and gave it to the Marines. In less than a week, the Marines expeditionary units built checkpoints all over the routes from Jarf al Sakhar toward us in Exanddryah. They secured the bridges in the Presidential Canal in South Baghdad and placed barbed wire in the small dirt roads between the major checkpoints crossing the main routes. I called those small dirt roads shortcuts to avoid the checkpoints. The U.S. Marines had done their share and more; the checkpoints disrupted the transfer of weapons while simultaneously thwarting the special groups' efforts to plant IEDs along supply routes. The mortar rounds decreased.

I took the Sheik's plan to its second phase and went out into the public. Silent heroes accompanied me: the American children who had donated hundreds of thousands of dollars to the Iraqi children. The mothers and fathers of these American children are my heroes: they were right there with me, their donations sitting in storage rooms, untouched until Sheik

Goodman advised me to become the conduit for communication with Iraqis in the area.

The Sheik's pioneering advice to my team for making contacts with the public became a tradition that is followed even today. We gave the Iraqi children what our little American heroes sent for them, and it was a success. Most Iraqi children dressed alike. Girls wore long, black gowns with long sleeves to cover their arms and hands and a scarf covering their heads; their faces did not have to be covered, though. The boys' gowns were khaki, blue, white or grey. Very few had Western-style pants or shirts. In school, the boys wore shoes, but the ones who rushed to meet us in the streets typically went barefoot. The quality of these children's clothing was also noticeably lower than that of the schoolchildren — their clothes were like rags, full of tears and covered in mud.

In the schools, teachers dressed in Western-style clothes. The men were clean shaven, with no beards, and very few of them spoke English. Most of them asked me if I spoke Russian, but I had to tell them no. I thought their questions were simply out of curiosity. We drove to every little elementary school and stood talking to the children and their teachers for hours. They asked for more coloring books, writing pads, and even for teddy bears, stuffed animals like Barney, cookies and candy bars. I held their hands and talked to them, and they did not treat me like a stranger — they behaved as though they had known me all their lives. The teachers asked for pens and lesson books, for crayons and markers and even powdered drink mixes like Kool-Aid. We asked the American children to donate these things, and our little heroes did what they could and provided their best. A few days later, we distributed these things to all the schools near the bases — Kool-Aid and all!

In less than a month, our reputation reached throughout Iraq. All the other bases were encouraged to go out to the schools and distribute items donated by America's smallest heroes. For weeks, Iraqi children ran as fast as they could to meet our HMMWVs when they saw us approaching their neighborhoods.

The men and women of Iraq asked for medicine. Diabetics especially needed it. We sent a huge amount of medical supplies to local clinics, all donated by the American people.

The healthy Iraqis asked for cigarettes. We had hundreds of cartons donated to the troops by Americans, but most of us did not smoke, so we gave them ours too. I had never before seen people light a fresh cigarette from one that was still burning — the Iraqis loved them!

We gained knowledge and experience by talking to the public. We began stopping in different neighborhoods every day to hold friendly conversations with the people. The people began to like us more and more; they began volunteering the names of those who planted IEDs on the roads and fired mortar rounds at us. They also gave us the names of people who operated in the Death Triangle. I am still proud of their hard work — I kept the Special Forces busy by collecting these names and putting them in my reports, which I submitted to the Marines.

The people also told me about what they needed. They wanted electricity more than anything — even medicine. They also wanted new bridges since most of them had been destroyed by the war.

The Marines asked me to tell Sheik Goodman to bring engineers for them to contract for local goods and services. I called him, and he asked me to give him a week to see what he could find. In less than a week, he brought us more than fifteen different engineers! The Marines felt blessed: they knew he would bring us some engineers, but not that many! The Marines had some projects on hand before Sheik Goodman had enabled them to operate in full capacity.

Everything went well. The road bombs decreased from about twenty a week to less than three per week. The mortar attacks decreased as well, from as many as six per week down to one. Yet I never found one weapon cache. I even asked some of the locals I knew well, but most of them had very little information.

I knew there must be many weapons in the area — this was, after all, the Death Triangle, where Hammurabi's Brigade was. This was where the Iraqi Army's weapons factory was located before we destroyed it in the twenty-one day war. I realized that I needed to talk to Sheik Goodman again.

I called the Sheik and he came. We sat for a long time, talking about his daughter, who was ill, and her medicine. We talked about the area in general, the great progress we had made with our different projects, and how he helped me turn my dreams into reality.

Finally, I asked him about the weapons and why no one would talk to me about them. He said, "Listen my friend.

There are a lot of weapons around here. There is a stash in every berm, every orchard, and every farm. All these weapons are stripped for plastics and placed inside of barrels or huge drums and buried underground. The people will not give them to you, but they will not use the weapons against you, either: they have stashed them to use to fight each other in the future."

I asked Sheik Goodman why the people wanted to fight each other. He paused for a while, and then looked at me. "You would not understand," he replied. He said there were a lot of reasons that he could not explain. "Try me," I replied. "You might be surprised." The Sheik asked me if I knew how long it had been since the Shiites were able to express themselves. I answered "Yes — since the Ottoman Empire." "Yes," he said.

"Never underestimate me just because I came from America," I said. "I know," the Sheik replied. Then he stated, "The time has come for the Shiites to rule Iraq. They will win by their majority. If democracy does not work, then the weapons will be dug out of the ground . . ."

I knew that Sheik Goodman spoke from his heart. I remembered what Saddam did to the Kurdish people in 1991 when we left him alive after the first Gulf War. Today, if the Shiite nation is oppressed under the new Iraqi government, they are determined not to let the same thing happen again.

I asked the Sheik if there was any possible solution, and he advised me to wait and see if the Shiites won the election; then we could offer to buy the weapons from them. He told me that most of the people in the Death Triangle were farmers, and that they had food — sheep, goats, cattle, even palm dates —

but they had no cash in their pockets. Therefore, some of them might feel comfortable enough after the election to sell the weapons to us for cash. When I inquired about trying to buy weapons before the election, he told me that it was a long shot, but that I could try. I thanked the Sheik and rushed to submit an urgent report.

I talked to people in the Marines about offering money for weapons collections, but it got me nowhere. Some highly intelligent commanders in Baghdad were happy with the idea: in the beginning, people surrendered a lot of dysfunctional weapons, and eventually, they surrendered the functioning ones, too. A few weeks later, the number of weapons collected increased. Weapons caches surfaced here and there. The U.S. Marines on my base were willing to try, but there was a particular Junior Officer opposed to the idea, and eventually, the attempt just died out altogether.

I was very happy. In my heart, I felt relieved and greatly appreciated Sheik Goodman. Things were so good that I felt blessed. I went out with my team. At our first stop outside the gate, we gave medicine to a sick child. We promised his mother we would return the next day with more; she thanked us, and we drove down the dirt road between the palm dates that reached into the sky. We entered the freeway, and after a mile reached an exit to the Swayrah freeway. Three miles up, it led to Dolaymi. We drove about three hundred yards off road to climb a steep hill. The view from this hill was a green field that stretched in front of us like a giant, natural mountain. I saw a few brick homes scattered among the green fields divided by strips of palm trees. The white of the homes contrasted beautifully with the dark green reflected by the palm leaves. The brown of the trees' bark made the homes appear to be surrounded by natural fences.

This hill was a good place to view the Dolaymi tribal area, a tribe that was aggressive toward us. They had attacked us by mortar rounds several times, so I was attempting to make friends among them.

A cloud of smoke not too far from the hill caught my attention. We saw two men and a woman standing next to a smoking oven outside their home. The woman was in her early sixties; dressed in a black gown, her head was covered in a black rag. She was standing next to a homemade clay oven built on the ground. It was small with a little dome on top, and I could see the oven's door from the top of the hill because its smoke was piercing the clear morning's sky. She had closed the oven's door with a piece of flat tin, but when she moved it to take out the bread, the smoke increased.

Her two sons stood next to her, talking and eating the fresh, hot bread. They were dressed in traditional white Arabian-style gowns. They did not appear to be carrying guns or any other kind of weapon, so I turned to the members of my team and asked them if they wanted to try some of her fresh bread. "Hell, yeah!" they replied! The smell rose to the hill where we were standing, and it smelled so good.

I turned and waved to the woman and her sons. They waved back, so I greeted them in Arabic. They all responded, *"Alycom alsalam"* which means "Peace be with you."

I stopped to speak to them in Arabic. They greeted me and my team and then I heard the woman instruct her sons to invite us in. She was cooking fresh bread. It was 8:30 A.M. and she

The aroma of fresh bread and the generosity of the Iraqi Bedouins. Even though the situation was bad and a lot of people hated us, some people still had beautiful hearts. We had gotten the message and we never went back to see them again, to avoid getting them hurt.

Nothing is safe from the road bombs. This ram is the luckiest ram in Iraq — he survived one. It almost cut his neck.

thought we might be hungry. I still marvel at the generosity of the local people — some of the team members tried the bread, including the female member of our team. The old woman asked me to translate for her, but as I was doing so, something caught my eye: there was a ram tied to the far side of the house, and half of his neck had no wool or skin. I asked the old woman what had happened to the ram, and she answered that the ram had survived a road bomb. Soon, all the members of my team were taking pictures of the ram, who was so scared by the cameras' flashes that he almost died of fear.

All of us were talking and laughing, joking around with each other, when we suddenly heard a loud bang. It was a sound known to every one of us: an IED had been detonated.

Immediately, I asked these local friends for permission to

leave. I also asked the old woman to accept my gift, but I practically had to beg her to take it before she would. After we had greeted each other, the woman took her last loaf from the oven and gave it to me. It was delicious. The loaf was so large that I held it in both hands, its roasted, brown crust covering its tender interior. I tore it into two pieces, and its aroma was lovely. Handing half to my other team member, I took a big bite.

Soon, every member of my team accepted his own loaf of bread from the woman. The ten of us ate as if we hadn't eaten in days! I translated their compliments to the old woman, who was happy that Americans were enjoying her homemade bread. I even told her son that he should bring her bread to the base to sell.

I decided to return the old woman's hospitality and generosity with a gift. I explained to her that I was not paying her for her gift to us, which would have been insulting, but that my gift was intended for her to buy extra spices and ingredients to bake with since we intended to return and eat more on our next visit. I wanted to beg her to take some money in good faith, but I knew that she would have been insulted.

We jumped in our HMMWVs and popped smoke, leaving a cloud of dust from the HMMWV's screaming engines. We headed to where we thought the road bomb had gone off and found that it had in fact detonated, but thankfully, no one, other than the man who had tried to plant it in the road, was killed.

He was splattered to pieces on the side of the road. Some of his flesh and bits of his clothes were hanging from the barbed wire fence. There was nothing left of him but his underarm. The bomb had left a big hole in the ground.

I traced his footsteps to see how he had come so close to the checkpoint without being seen. It seemed to me that he had never walked since the vehicle dropped him fifty yards east of the same road where he had tried to plant the IED.

A vehicle had dropped him and left. He had crawled inside the ditch that was parallel to the road — the low ditch and the high grass beside it had concealed him well. He must have had the bomb tied to his back, then had crawled about fifty yards before reaching a hole that he had dug earlier next to the curve of the road. Then he must have dropped the bomb or pulled a wire accidentally. He must have been close to the bomb when it went off because the impact left his remains splattered everywhere along the barbed wire.

What turned out to be a bad day for him could have also been a bad day for us.

That same day, we went on a patrol mission with the Marines to a nearby town of Dayarah. A senior staff member of our team had arranged the mission with the Marines. The purpose was to look for the people who were planting the IEDs at night. I was not aware of this arrangement and was very angry about our participation in this mission. The person who had arranged it knew that our command in Baghdad ordered us to cease our missions outside the base after 5 P.M.

The mission itself did not serve any purpose concerning the IEDs or those planting the bombs because we had reported to the Marines many times that the IEDs were being planted in the early morning, around 4:30 to 5:00 A.M. during the

He set the road bomb to kill us, but God took him first, and he splattered onto the barbed wire fence and everywhere. Only his underarm was found in one piece.

Pointing to the finger tip and skin.

Muslims' morning prayers. Sometimes the bombs were planted on the roads between 7:00 to 9:00 A.M., such as this morning when the man planting the bomb had blown himself up.

The mission was a bad move. At 6 P.M. we had our four HMMWVs lined up behind three Marine strikers' armored vehicles. We changed this configuration so that a Marine striker led the convoy. My vehicle was second, followed by another vehicle from my team, and a second Marine striker was stationed behind this vehicle. Two other HMMWVs were placed behind our two last vehicles, and the third Marine striker was stationed at the end of the convoy.

The convoy commander ordered the movement and all seven armored vehicles proceeded through the base's East gate. We disappeared into the night. It was dark, and we drove without lights. The dust made the visibility poor. The absence of night vision made everyone on the team angry — the senior officer had arranged this mission before receiving night vision goggles that would have enabled us to see in the dark. So we drove on, upset and angry.

Dayarah was not a friendly place. Located in the middle of a thousand irrigation canals, it only had one paved road leading in and out of town. It was absolutely idiotic to conduct a mission like this; to go up against your enemy at night without night vision and without an alternative retreat route.

We drove slowly through a green cornfield. From time to time we would run into a vehicle coming in the opposite direction and the convoy would have to swerve to the side of the road in order to let the vehicle pass. The convoy was extremely vulnerable to attack: we had no place to turn around before we reached the town. We would have to take our chances on a dirt road, possibly sinking in the mud created by the irrigation canals.

Reaching Dayarah, we entered the shopping area. We passed a few scattered single-clay chambers and clay booths filled with local merchandise such as food and clothing. To my surprise, the mission commander ordered the convoy to stop and buy anything they might need. The little local market was lit with gas lamps that were likely stolen from our own supply convoys. We parked our vehicles to the sides of the clay rooms and exited to shop.

This stop attracted the attention of every potential enemy in the area. People with cell phones transmitted news of our arrival to those outside of Dayarah. We had even used the lights on our vehicles to find parking in the market, attracting as much attention as possible.

After shopping in near darkness with people who really didn't want to see us, we drove between two rows of mud shacks into Dayarah, leaving most of the shoppers behind us to roam around in the only exit we could use after this unknown mission was accomplished. Traveling only two more blocks, we stopped again. The mission commander told us to police the western side of the neighborhood, but not to pass the school. The Marines would police the eastern side. I asked why we were policing the neighborhood, but he just shrugged. Unsatisfied with this response, I asked again: why did he arrange for our participation in this mission? He told me that he had been told to look for people who planted IEDs in the roads.

I told the senior officer that he was wrong for accepting a mission without a written statement to study or discuss with his staff before executing the mission. Did he know that the market gate was the only way in and out of town?

We divided our teams into two-man patrols. I chose my team member and proceeded to walk toward the school. We left two team members to guard the vehicles, each standing behind the long range machine guns. The mission commander told us to come back to the vehicles within an hour.

Half way down an alley, a black dog started barking at me and my buddy. "What are we looking for?" my teammate asked. I told him that we were looking for the guy who shot us dead. He laughed and said "I feel stupid." I laughed, too. "That makes two of us," I said.

"Why in the hell are we wandering around in a town that does not value our troops' protection or well-being?" he asked. "How can you even see a hundred yards from here? How can I even see a person twenty yards away from here in the middle of the palm trees?"

"All your questions are valid," I said. "You are a walking target today. If either of us dies, we're not serving America or moving this war forward, not even making one inch of progress. Our deaths would be the result of stupidity, poor planning, and a failure to follow Baghdad Command's orders!"

"This is a bad day," he said.

"You'd better believe it," I replied.

At this point, the black dog that had barked at us was becoming really agitated. Suddenly, two other dogs came running out behind us. I put down my M16 and took my 9mm out of my holster. The two dogs behind us were getting too close. Then I remembered an old trick my brother taught me: if a dog comes running toward you fast, lean down to the ground as if you are picking up a stone and then pretend you are throwing the stone at the dog. So when the two dogs were less than twenty yards away, I did this, but this time I actually did pick up a stone and hit one of the dogs on its head. It fell on its back from the shock and surprise of it. The other dog tripped on the first dog and also fell on its back. Both dogs stood up and ran away, screeching. A guy stretched his head out from behind a fence and asked us if everything was okay.

"Everything is fine," I said. The black dog that started this mess had also run away by then.

"Why are you wasting your time here?" the man asked us. "There is nothing here other than guard dogs, and you might get bit by them. Or by snakes," he warned us.

"I feel so stupid," my teammate said again.

"Join the club," I answered. "That man just called us stupid," I told him.

"Do you want some water?" the man asked us.

"No, thank you," I answered, embarrassed.

We proceeded, looking around the dark, empty alleys until we ran into a dead end. Circling, we came back the same way and changed roads.

We saw a person waving at us at the end of an alley. "Be careful," I told my buddy. "There is a guy waving at us, wanting us to go to him. It might be a trap."

Slowly, carefully, we walked toward him. After getting a few yards closer, I realized it was a Marine waving. When we made it over to him, he told us that the Base Commander had ordered the termination of the mission and ordered us back to the base. It was 10 P.M. by then, so I understood the Base Commander's concern — the mission had been plain stupid in the first place. All an insurgent had to do was park an eighteen wheeler in the gate of the road and block us inside Dayarah, then hunt us one by one. Without any other exit or night vision goggles, we wouldn't have been able to fight back. The insurgents could have had a successful attack, and each one of us knew this to be true. Eventually, the senior officer was questioned about accepting this mission, which was led by a kid who was a Marine corporal.

9

THE BAD DAY,
THE SETBACK DAY:
JULY, 2004

Everything was so right. Our relationships with schoolteachers and children, the local clinics and the people in surrounding neighborhoods were strong — that is, until Saddam showed up on television. It was the first day of his trial.

Saddam's appearance changed the attitudes of those around us forever. The day was a total setback from everything we had worked for.

The morning began as usual. We loaded the candy, toys, toiletries and cigarettes onto our trucks and left the base to distribute them to people in the neighborhood. From the moment we left the base, however, it was obvious that something was wrong. There was no traffic; no pedestrians either. No children were playing outside their homes.

We drove through three neighborhoods, and not one child came running toward us as they usually did. We were silent, but as I looked at my team members, their eyes told it all. Something was not right.

Far off in the distance, we saw one family on a cabbage farm harvesting their crop, a young man loading cabbage into baskets to put onto his truck. He was dressed in regular pants with a leather belt and brown and grey long sleeved shirt and white sneakers. His father, who appeared to be in his early forties, was dressed in the long traditional Arab gown without a collar. He had a white rag on his head that was secured with a black tie. Iraqis and Saudis call this head covering a *"qutrah."* The mother looked to be in her late thirties and was dressed in a long black gown. The upper part of the gown was folded and tied at the waist and her head was covered with a green rag.

Their little girl was dressed like her mother, but her long, black hair was showing. It fell behind her shoulders and reached all the way down her back. She was about nine or ten years old. Both the mother and the daughter had sickles in their hands and wide baskets full of cabbage. The father held a long digging tool and a sickle in his other hand. We drove toward them to socialize and find out where everybody had gone.

We dismounted, and I shook hands with them in greeting. We had a good time communicating with them in Arabic. Everyone responded and was pleasant. Then the young man, Ziyad, asked me why Saddam was still alive. Why had we not killed him?

I suddenly knew that was the reason the streets were

empty. Saddam's appearance had something to do with everyone else's disappearance.

I told the young man that we could not just kill Saddam. We left him alive so the Iraqis could take him to court and prosecute him; they could kill him if they found him guilty. The young man responded that *everyone* already knew Saddam was guilty! "He killed a lot of people without any trials," Ziyad argued: "Why should he be given one?"

I answered that Saddam should be given a trial because the Iraqis were better than he was. Saddam should be treated the way everyone should be treated, and that meant giving him the opportunity for a fair trial.

Ziyad said that was a big mistake. He spoke from his heart. Even though he was just a teenager, he echoed what every Iraqi citizen seemed to feel that day.

This ordinary farmer told us not to come to his farm after Saddam's first appearance on TV. He said he was not afraid of anyone, but he did not want to see us around.

Ordinary people did not want to see us after Saddam appeared on TV for the first day of his court trial.

I asked again why there were no people in the street, and Ziyad answered that they were afraid of Saddam. I reassured him that Saddam was in prison, in handcuffs, but Ziyad told me that Saddam's secret police (the Udai) still had weapons and that now they wanted revenge.

I tried to explain that Saddam, his sons and the Udai secret police were not effective any more, but Ziyad told me this was not true. He told me that Udai's orphans were vicious: they would cut out people's tongues with sharp blades and shoot people in the back of the head with guns; that was why no one was out today.

I asked him why he was out today, and he answered that he was not afraid because he had an AK-47 in his truck.

I wondered if Ziyad was right about allowing Saddam to appear on television.

That same day, we swung by the neighborhood elementary school to give out candy and toys, but to my surprise the principal and teachers asked us not to come back again. The school was in a neighborhood dominated by Sunnis, and Udai's orphans were around. The principal told me that most of the schoolchildren were Shiites, and that he appreciated our kindness, but for the sake of the children and their families, we should never come back. I promised him that we would not, but I still gave him the boxes of goods we brought for the children. "Consider it our gift," I said, and we shook hands.

I never saw him or the schoolchildren again.

Similar instances occurred with all the other schools, medical centers, and local clinics.

The weapon returns for money also stopped. Our friendly relationships with the communities slowly ended.

A few days after Saddam's first day of trial, the Marine checkpoint in the gold hill called our team to interrogate some insurgent groups that had constructed a fake checkpoint. We went there and saw that the checkpoint had been built under a bridge; sand bags had been stacked to create a wall that stretched from the ground to the underside of the bridge. Two young Marine Lieutenants were in charge of the platoon operating in the checkpoint. There were also two groups of Marines guarding each side of the bridge, living in the shelter that resembled homelessness. On the south side of the wall, soldiers had written "TOMBSTONE" above where the Marines stood.

One mortar was set up on the South side of the bridge, and there were two soldiers sitting next to it. I took the lead and started talking to these two guys.

This water hole is the only source of water for many families.

"Who gave you the right to set up an illegal checkpoint and harass civilians?" I asked.

"It was a mistake," one of them responded," but we did it to protect the Shiites who travel to Karbala and Najaf through the Sunni dominated land."

The Marine Lieutenant told them that he would arrest them if he found them conducting a fake checkpoint, but he let them go before we returned to the base. We sat down and talked about the town of Tombstone in the old West and cowboys like Wyatt Earp. We would talk about anything to pass the time and get our minds off of this madness.

At the base, I was changing clothes when I heard an IED go off. "Oh no!" yelled one of our team members; "it's in the direction of Tombstone!"

I knew this was true. Everyone stopped what they were doing. We stood silent for a moment. Suddenly, we heard a

This family drinks water from the water hole shown on page 84.

high caliber machine gun rattling loudly. Then we heard two other explosions, and everything went dead.

Soon we heard the all clear on the radio. It had been an IED at Tombstone, followed by an RPG and PKC attack, but the Marines had it under control. A convoy coming from Saudi was ambushed and Senior Officer James had been killed. His convoy passed our base while we were parking next to the tent.

At 6 A.M. the next morning, my informant came running to tell me who was responsible for the attack. The guard at the gate called me over the radio, and I told him to escort my informant to the tent.

My informant told me that Hussein Abu Ali, who lived in Mahmudyah, had killed Senior Officer James. He drew a map of Hussein's house for me and gave me a description of the man.

I thanked my informant and told him to come back and see me in three hours so that I could give him a weapons permit. He would need it in order to carry a weapon to protect himself and his family.

I submitted my report to the Marine Command, and they distributed the description of Hussein Abu Ali to all the Marine checkpoints in the area. At 3 P.M., Hussein came to cross the Marine checkpoint, wearing the same shirt that my informant had described him in. The Marines successfully arrested him, and I felt like SSG James's could finally rest in heaven.

Hussein cried like a child during his interrogation. He was later released to Iraqi authorities with a recommendation for execution.

That same week, Ezzat Ibrahim Al Duri, number six out of fifty in Saddam's cabinet and godfather to Saddam, attacked us in Tikrit. Ezzat's attacks, both in Tikrit and in Biji, were not successful, but they were an expression of his loyalty to Saddam Hussein. Ezzat collapsed in the Tikrit attack and was taken to a nearby medical center.

We killed more than 150 members of his group that day.

Ezzat was lying on a stretcher in the medical center for two hours after the attacks on American bases were over. He later announced to many people that the Americans could have arrested him if they had looked in the only medical center in Tikrit, and that was the only chance Americans had of catching him alive.

Ezzat Ibrahim immediately allied himself with Zarqawi, ending the honeymoon between the special groups, Shiites and Sunnis. Zarqawi's special groups went back to Al Mahadi's army, where they belonged.

What began instead was a new honeymoon between Ezzat Ibrahim and Zarqawi: they called themselves the Iraqi National Unity (changed to different names later) and established a political office next to Al Yarmook hospital in Baghdad. Zarqawi posed as a tribal representative of Iraq, the same party held by Ahmed Chalabi until today. Ahmed Chalabi is the Iraqi who misled the Bush administration about the weapons of mass destruction that provoked them into going to war with Iraq. Ahmed Chalabi is an acquaintance and a close friend of Dr. Ajami who is a TV news commentator in the U.S. concerning Arab countries.

Zarqawi brought in two former colonels from Saddam's intelligence to hold his administration in the INU. He also brought in two assassins, the Zaydan brothers Hassan and Fadil. Ezzad Ibrahim brought in Dr. Nihro al Kassanzan, a lecturer at Babylon University in Al Hillah, as his representative in the INU and began organizing the tribes of Iraq against multinational forces and the government of Iraq. Ezzat wasted no time after seeing that Saddam was still alive. Even though Ezzat Ibrahim's honeymoon with Zarqawi had started, he also had his distant cousin Ahmed Al Ahmadi and seven hundred of the former military intelligence officers in standby to be planted in the new Iraqi army as a Plan B.

Dr. Nihro contacted all the Sheiks of Iraq under the instruction of Ezzat and assembled them in a Zigzaganiyah mansion in Al Hillah, then took them in minibuses to Sulaymanyah, near Iran's borders, where Ezzat lived.

Dr. Nihro knew about the Saddam mansions, Zigzaganiyahs from Hassan Zaydan, and the secret service officer in charge of Saddam's special hideout. Hassan Zayden had all the keys to these hideouts, and he gave keys to three of

Dr. Nihro Kissanzan, the right-hand man of Ezzat Ibrahim Al Duri, number six man on the wanted list, was posing as a legal secretary general of Iraqi National Unity.

these places (Zigzaganiyahs, mansions) to Dr. Nihro to use as lodging for sheiks traveling from Hillah in the South to Sulaymanyah in the Northeast of Baghdad. Dr. Nihro's routes were from Hillah to Dawrah, where Tariq Aziz, Saddam's right-hand man, used to live. The Zigzaganiyah was not too far from the military clothing factory that was destroyed during the liberation of Iraq. It was on the Hillah-Ramady freeway. Dr. Nihro kept the sheiks' convoys in Dawrah overnight, and then took them the following day to spend a night in a Zigzaganiyah in Tikrit. On the third day, the convoy would arrive in Sulaymanyah, which is in northeast Iraq, near the border of Iran. All the routes were secured by Zarqawi's militia.

Ezzat Ibrahim would meet every sheik's convoy with great hospitality, and then instruct the sheiks to kill the infidels and occupiers as well as the Iraqi police forces and Army forces created to help the occupiers. He told the sheiks to take anything belonging to the former government of Iraq; to open former government facilities and take the vehicles, furniture, computers, and anything else they could find. He instructed them to break down the doors to all the banks and take the money because the Iraqis running the new Iraq were nothing but immigrant thieves who came with the occupiers to steal their money and their oil.

Ezzat himself stole billions of dollars from the Iraqis which he hid in barrels in Sulaijnanyah. He also gave each sheik hundreds of U.S. dollars before their convoys departed to Hillah. Hundreds of these convoys met Ezzat after the day Saddam appeared on television.

Tribal sheiks returned to begin their wars on the police and the checkpoints of Iraq's Army bases. Police units became targets all over Iraq, but Al Anbar province and Dayalah were hit hard first.

Zarqawi had every new graduate from the police forces exterminated if they came from Jordan. He left their corpses on the roads to rot and be eaten by wild animals. After the day Saddam appeared on television, the Sunni Bathists who had told sad stories to the recruiters and joined the Iraqi Army or police, rose again to pull another trick from their hats: they started a war of assassinations.

The war of assassinations was the spark that ignited the Iraqi Civil War which our administration has never fully admitted.

Police officers killed by Zarqawi's lieutenant on the Death Highway.

Zarqawi's attack on the newly graduated police officers coming from Jordan on the Death Triangle freeway was beyond description.

10

IRAQI CIVIL WAR OF ASSASSINATION:

DECEMBER, 2004 – SEPTEMBER 2007

The war of assassination was a private, internal war carried out by the Sunni (former Bathists) to exterminate Iraqi Civil Defense Core elements (ICDC) and to take over the commanding positions. It was a war driven by desire for power: ICDC were the early Iraqi National Guard units that had developed into the Iraqi Army and police units of today. ICDC was not made up of honorable or remarkable people, but they were the only people available at that time.

The ICDC was composed of three Iraqi elements. The first group was enormous: it consisted of Iraqis with low-level educations. The second group was the lowest enlisted elements from the former Iraqi Army. The third group was huge as well; it consisted of the criminals Paul Brimmer released from prison before he gave Iraq over to the transitional government. The combination of these three groups was a recipe for disaster.

Some ICDC members soon acquired guns and badges and began driving around Iraqi neighborhoods, targeting rich Iraqis. They would force them to give over their money and their homes or face being burned alive. Many Iraqis complained about the ICDC's misdeeds, We also suffered their wrath. At night they shot mortar rounds at our multinational bases and FOBs; they planted IEDs along supply routes again, but these were close to their checkpoints in their sectors of roads. They also helped the insurgents by using their credentials to pass the weapons brought through checkpoints.

The sheiks of the tribes did not have a problem sending tribal members to ICDC checkpoints and bases, where attacks became deadly.

Sunni Bathists found great opportunities to shoot high ranking officers in the back in every tribal insurgent counterattack. Sometimes ICDC officers were assassinated on their way home.

The Sunni Bathists were able to dominate the existing ICDC leadership, but their hunger for power was not yet fulfilled. Their expansion sparked the civil war; Sunni Bathists started to assassinate Shiite officers in the ICDC. Shiites became aware of this, and the Iraqi government demanded that we segregate the units into Shiite and Sunni groups. We complied with this decision, which seemed fine, but it did not solve the problem of the secret assassinations. In many ways, it was the worst decision made by the Iraqi government because it widened the gap between Sunnis and Shiites.

Soon the government took this decision to segregate Sunni units from Shiite units even further: the government told us to completely move the Sunni units to Sunni dominant areas and to move Shiite units to areas dominated by Shiites. This was when the real civil war started. Criminals were involved so it was out of control. The only rules to this new criminal war belonged to the imaginations of those who enjoyed it most: Al Hussayn's special groups.

11

THE CIVIL WAR/
CRIMINAL WAR

Moving the Sunni and Shiites to their dominant areas created a social problem. Sunnis who were minorities in Shiite areas started to voluntarily move to Sunni dominant areas; Shiites did the same. Soon, harassment began. The Sunni minorities who preferred to stay in their homes because of attachments to family or their area's history were forced to leave, and the same fate met Shiites in Sunni dominant areas.

Next, the Shiite special groups of Al Hussein's brigade declared jihad on the Sunnis in general and began bombing temples and mosques in Sunni dominant areas. The criminal war was full-blown — massive immigration of Sunnis and Shiites to their respective areas began, and there was panic in the streets. Looting, raping, and killing became commonplace. Mass graves were found everywhere. Each group learned how to make car bombs. If the Sunnis detonated a car bomb in a Shiite mosque, the Shiites would detonate two car bombs in a Sunni dominant area, such as a marketplace. Sunnis would hunt, kidnap and kill Shiites who battered the Sunnis during deportation from their homes. Beheadings occurred by the hundreds. They were filmed and shown on televisions news channels. Corpses were dumped in public garbage cans. Sometimes bodies without heads were left in the middle of a street or on a bridge with a note attached saying "Sunnis meet" or "Shiites meet." Beheading became a public spectacle done in front of women and children. It got so bad that most of the wealthier, non-aggressive Iraqis fled to Jordan, Syria, the United Arab Emirates, and even Australia. Unauthorized checkpoints were placed everywhere, and no one from the Iraqi government could pass through Shiite dominant areas without dealing with Al Mahadi's army; similarly, no government official could pass through Sunni dominant areas without somehow dealing with Zarqawi and Sunni groups.

The young Iraqi government had lost control over the Sunnis and Shiites. Hundreds of political parties appeared: Islamic parties, Sader parties, former Bathist parties, etc. The Bathists were unable to break through and take vital positions in the new government, but they took positions in the Ministry of the Interior, the Secret Service, or in Foreign Affairs.

The Kurds were able to seize the lands that had been stolen from them throughout the centuries. They cut their own borders and established their own checkpoints. They controlled their own portion of the pipeline and started to smuggle oil to Syria and Turkey. They also created their own semi-independent Kurdistan country with its own government.

Sunnis had taken the mid-central area of Iraq from Tikrit to Baghdad and made it their own. They also built checkpoints through the Ramadi and the Abu Ghraib freeways. They charged tolls to every Iraqi oil convoy passing through to Syria.

Shiites had done what no other party thought about: they fought the government's army and took control of the entire Iraqi pipeline. They also took by force all of the internal fueling stations and refineries. Al Hussein Brigade special group leaders organized oil smuggling to Turkey and Syria by using the former government's gasoline tankers. They basically controlled the entire Iraqi economy. Moreover, they controlled the movements of government officials since their vehicles had to be fueled by Al Mahadi's army elements. While the Kurdish were busy building Kurdistan and the Sunnis occupied different government positions, Al Mahadi's army had stolen the wealth out from under them. But there was still more corruption.

Saddam's governing system was based on iron-fisted communism. The administrative system was very simple and effective at controlling the people; therefore, Al Mahadi's army took over the former government's style and applied it in order to control Iraq. The country was divided into provinces, which were divided further into judicial districts; these districts were subdivided into sectors. Al Mahadi's army had established their illegal checkpoints in Shiite dominant areas, not to collect toll fees but to control entire sectors' leadership. They killed every uniformed person working for the government and every government official who was not Shiite. Slowly, they took their Shiite areas from the young Iraqi government sector by sector.

Soon they advanced to take the weak Sunni tribal areas. Shiites succeeded at taking most of the Sunni dominated areas around Baccubah and the pipelines in Kurdish lands. Shiites' boldness and Al Hussein's special groups' aggressiveness led to new problems that linger in Iraq even today and will remain as long as Al Hussein's special groups are not controlled. Since Zarqawi was the only Sunni Militia in the North, Sunnis came to an agreement with him to fight Shiites who declared *jihad* on them.

Then a war based on hate and revenge began among armed gangs.

12

THE GANG WAR:

JANUARY 2005 – TODAY

Shiite success against the government in claiming their land made them attempt to take Sunni land inhabited by a Shiite majority. Shiite Al Mahadi's army armed every Shiite willing to bring the Shiites glory as the early Islamists had done. Shiites prepared themselves to avenge Al Hussein's death and mutilation and to take the Sunni's land.

On the other hand, Sunnis were armed by Zarqawi and the Islamic party. Former Bathists also aided in arming them by stealing weapons from their army units. Both parties were ready to fight, but they did not consider the fact that they had armed hundreds of criminals that Paul Brimmer had released — criminals who had no commitment to Al Hussein, the Americans, or to Iraq.

These criminals were just praying to God for weapons,

and they got their weapons and free transportation in order to carry out their own message and deliver it to Iraq. While Al Hussein and the Sunnis were fighting for glory, the criminals, both Sunnis and Shiites, started their own war on civilian Iraqis who had imprisoned them in the past. In every neighborhood, *compardres* were driving around, looking for the judges who had sentenced them to jail. When they found them, they killed them and their families. They hunted down lawyers and police members who had played a part in their arrests and prosecutions. Nothing could stop these criminals.

The criminals got the opportunity to breed new terror among the people of Iraq. Utilities workers were killed for not connecting electricity to their neighborhoods quickly enough; irrigation workers were slain for not fixing canals. Soon the criminals, both Sunni and Shiite, began to kidnap their own people to deliver each other for revenge. Some went to Syria, Turkey, the United Arab Emerites, Iran or Jordan to kidnap people and bring them back to Iraq and sell them for revenge. It did not take long before the criminals took over the entire country. They made their war on blood against the leadership of both Sunnis and Shiites.

Mogtada al Sader kept his hierarchy because the criminals could not touch him; Zarqawi also kept his position because he was the biggest gun of them all. Zarqawi was declared a prince by Osama Bin Laden, a title he retained until his death.

The criminal war did not stop there, however. They progressively occupied every government position. Educated Sunnis and Shiites took government positions in their respective areas, and the criminally dominated government of Iraq was born. Iraq regressed to something worse than it had been in the past: the corruption returned on an even larger scale. Bribery, theft, embezzlement — every corrupt action one can dream of became commonplace. The Iraqi government was completely out of control, and it became the most hated enemy of the people. Sunni political parties did not agree with the government, and al Sader's party did not want to deal with the tribes of Iraq because they were difficult to communicate with regarding politics.

One thing didn't change: every one of the parties attacked us with mortars and set IEDs on our roads. The gang attacks on civilians were also great. Sometimes they attacked civilians on our bases.

I decided to find a way to fight the criminal gangs. Every government leader and the multinational forces came to realize that we were no longer just fighting Zarqawi and al Sader. We were fighting criminal gangs, whose only intent was exacting pure revenge, then gaining power and control over the Iraqi government.

It was impossible to fight every Iraqi walking around — we didn't know who the enemy was because the criminal gangs were everywhere, appearing and disappearing as they wished. The Iraqi people were paranoid and scared, and most of our former friends stopped coming to see us. Informants were nowhere to be found: the penalty for meeting with us was beheading. The criminal gangs were raising hell in Sunni and Shiite neighborhoods, sometimes shooting hundreds of mortar rounds on our bases.

I decided to talk to Sheik Goodman to see if he could help

us to control these criminal gangs. His experience as a colonel working in intelligence under Saddam might, I thought, have given him insight and knowledge into the situation. I invited him to talk, and we sat for a long time discussing the situation. Sheik Goodman looked into my eyes for quite a long time before speaking.

"The gang problem is so big," he said. "It is bigger than the Americans, bigger than the Iraqi government, bigger than the Iraqis themselves." He looked at the ceiling of my tent, then at me. He shook his head from left to right and asked me as politely as he could why we had emptied the prisons of these criminals in the first place.

I told him that I had no answer for him. I told him that Paul Brimmer needed to address that question because both the Iraqis and the Americans wanted an answer.

He asked me again why we had let tribal sheiks sponsor the people we detained as criminals who were convicted by the multinational forces, the Iraqi government and Iraqi justices.

Earlier, we had started to recruit Iraqi civilians in the ICDC, and they were not the best quality of people for the job. They were mostly uneducated criminals, and the ICDC groups became a disaster. ICDC forces threatened and robbed people, stealing money.

We came up with an idea that we thought was good and noble. We asked the tribal sheiks to bring well educated tribal members to take charge of their territories. The plan worked very well, and soon the sheiks discovered that we trusted them to help secure their own domain. They became corrupted and accepted money to write sponsorship letters that released detainees from detention facilities. We had given the sheiks authority to write the sponsorship letters and to be responsible for their own tribal members' criminal activities after their release. Theirs was a sharp betrayal to our trust and good intentions.

Sheik Goodman informed me that during Saddam's regime, the tribal sheiks were nobody. Most of them sold cigarettes in Baghdad at the East gate. He said that it was a good idea to ask them to bring educated, responsible Iraqis to join the service branches, but that giving them power to write sponsorships had been our mistake; it was too much power for the sheiks to handle. He then paused and admitted that it was not our mistake after all— we did not know enough about the Iraqis. We tried to do something smart, but didn't know what we were getting into.

I again asked him what we could do about the gangs. He looked at me deeply and replied, "Listen, my friend. The gangs are the government of Iraq now. To deal with the gangs, you will have to replace the entire government of Iraq, including the best friends of the Americans.

Abdullaziz Al Hakim is the top lieutenant and the founder of the superior counsel of the Islamic revolution, many of whose party members returned from their exile in Iran. Ahmed Chalabi, the founder of Iraqi National Conference, returned; party members had returned from their exile in Iran and Europe. Ibrahim Al Jafari, the head of Hizb Al Daawah party members had also returned from thier exile in Iran. Soon to be the man in charge of Iraq; Nuri Maliki, the commander of the Al Daawah military branch had returned from his Iranian exile; Bayan Jabor, the commander of Bader forces (the political branch of the superior counsel of the Islamic revolution) was back from Iran. The Mahadi army special groups were now bouncing back and forth between Maliki and Mugtada with no real control over them out there.

Then he said, "If you can take a diamond from the hands of an armed thief, and you don't have a weapon, you can take Iraq and give it back to Iraqis." Sheik Goodman said that every politician had his own security guard — "you could say 'security gang' " — and also that we should terminate the local Iraqi contractors who had successfully survived the gang wars and who created their own security guards. He said that the local contractors had compromised with the gangs.

He told me that the present Iraqi government officials in parliament or in the provinces had gotten direct control over the new Iraqi development projects' budgets. They controlled the vendors and bidding for contracts, and these contracts were given to friends and families of the politicians; some of them were criminals with companies that looked legitimate on paper, but were corrupt politicians' families or friends. Then the contracts would be sold for half the price to other companies to be built. These people were becoming wealthy without doing any work whatsoever.

He said that a lot of people were making profits at the expense of honest Iraqis who believed in democracy. The good Shiites and Sunnis were slowly being pushed out of the government and were succeeded by Al Hussein's brigade gangs. He told me that Mugtada was nothing other than an honest, confused young victim, just like all the other Iraqis.

Sheik Goodman emphasized that America needed to stop releasing the detainees involved in attacks on military bases and multinational bases, that we needed to keep them in detention for at least six months and then release them to Iraqi courts to be interrogated by law enforcement officers from independent areas. "Do not hand Shiite criminals to the Shiite courts or Sunni criminals to Sunni courts!" he exclaimed. "Revoke the sponsorship release letters from sheiks. Contracts should not be controlled by the Iraqi government or by the governments of local providences.

"Local companies which had received contracts of any kind and sold them to other companies to do the work should be forbidden from bidding on future contracts," he advised. As he spoke, he counted the issues on his fingers, folding down a finger each time he raised a point. He looked me in the eyes again and suggested that Americans must come up with a plan to protect their informants, even if it meant moving them onto bases along with their family members.

Finally, he told me that Americans should not share any intelligence with the Iraqi government or with any person, civilian or military, and to make their missions secret.

I was quiet. I let Sheik Goodman talk. I wanted him to give me his honest opinion. I had no idea that the Iraqi's money was being stolen from them by their own friends and relatives: the politicians. He told me a lot of things that our commanders could not possibly have control over, such as sharing intelligence and selling contracts.

I asked him what else we could do. There were so many

things he said that we just simply could not do. He smiled and said, "You cannot do what Saddam did, either. This was never a problem for Saddam." Saddam had a perfect control mechanism: the Mukhtars controlled the neighborhoods. FBs facilities, building security and police could detain any person the Mukhtars asked them to arrest. Local Army unit commands received and detained those detained by the FBs police. Local sector judges prosecuted those imprisoned by local army units and sent them to main prisons for a long time; sometimes forever. Saddam's Bathist party was the overall representative authority in each province. No one dared to make a mistake.

Finally, Sheik Goodman gave me something to think about: he told me that America must face the truth and prepare to fight the gangs in every neighborhood in Iraq. He said that these criminal gang members had become heroes among the Iraqis and that no one was willing to stand up to them. The criminals had portrayed themselves as freedom fighters against the occupation. They punished by death anyone who stood in their way.

He told me that the structure of the geography of Iraq was easy — Saddam had made the provinces, each of which had a number of sectors with a few Mukhtar "community leaders." He thought that the Mukhtars should be recruited by the Americans to control these communities again. This was important because they knew everyone in their community and could easily identify strangers hiding in their neighborhoods, or in hotels and motels. He said $400 to $500 U.S. would make each Mukhtar happy to protect his own community from the strangers, but the Mukhtars would have to be protected. Therefore, FBs should be recruited to safeguard the Mukhtars and their communities because both would automatically become targets for the gangs since they accepted employment by us. Communities should be policed for weapons immediately, and then every city and province would become safe. If we did a good job protecting them, all of Iraq would eventually be freed from the gangs.

Sheik Goodman also said that the Mukhtars knew where Iraqi weapons were hidden and who had hidden them. The Mukhtars were the key to solving the gang problem, but they must be properly protected before we even tried to convince them to work for us.

Many of the Mukhtars were already employed by Zarqawi and his top lieutenants. A lot of them were employed by the criminal gangs. We must find a way to provide security for them, and that will be the difficult part.

I understood Sheik Goodman's solution to the problem. He was a product of his environment. He lived with these issues every single day. He knew how things were done in the past and saw what had become of things today. His solution might have seemed easy, but it was against our policy to provide protection for the Mukhtars and local Iraqis.

One of the most damaging factors to our success was our failure to secure the safety of the Iraqi citizens; our failure to protect local translators, informants and the local contractors. If we found an article in our policy that gave us the opportunity to protect and secure our local workers, we could win this war immediately. Iraq could be restored in less than a year. Communities would be safe and free from gang control with the help of these knowledgeable Mukhtars. However, the FBs were the most powerful armed security group during Saddam's time, and they could do the same job today, but for better pay. In the past, FBS were paid $90,000 Iraqi dinars, equal to about $60 U.S. per month. $500 U.S. would make them happy and more prosperous.

I also understand our decision making was too slow in contrast to the events taking place in Iraq. Restoring sector after sector was a good idea, but the time involved would keep our troops in Iraq for years. The U.S. government would have to discuss the plan with Americans and the Congress. Everything would take a lot of time and money.

I thanked Sheik Goodman and told him I would call again after my trip to Babylon. I wanted to give him a personal gift to remember our friendship and show him how much I appreciated him. He smiled and shook my hand. The last words Sheik Goodman said to me were to "be safe." I smiled and responded automatically to him, without thinking. Two

We have been mortared from this location many times. It is not too far from the Beduins' tent site.

We were shot at from here by mortars. It was next to impossible to see the shooters from here.

days after our encounter, an incident happened that made me realize that I could not take his words for granted.

I could have died on October 5, 2004 at 6:18 P.M. It was like that song by Nat King Cole: "Unforgettable in every way." I woke up early that day and went to use the single portable bathroom that stood to the north of my tent, and then brushed my teeth outside the tent while everyone else was sleeping. The day began with a mild heat from the sun that pierced through the eastern horizon. The sun's rays were shielded by a few clouds and by palm trees that surrounded the base in all directions.

A bird was singing in the palm tree not too far from me. As I lifted my head to search for it, I thought to myself, "There are still some pretty things around here." Finally, I saw it: it was blue with a tiny red beak. It was so pretty. It did not see me because it was facing the other way, which made me glad because I didn't want it to fly away.

A few leaves and scraps of paper were floating in the wind at the wall of the tent. One of the local translators waved at me from the other tent on his way to the bathroom. I finished brushing my teeth and went inside to put on my uniform. I put the pistol in the holster that hung on the chest of my body armor and went, alone, to have my breakfast. On my way to the dining facility I saw the chaplain coming toward me. I waved at him and he waved back. I went inside and saw that the room was packed with Marines. Standing in line, I noticed that the people serving us were from India. They had strong accents, but I understood them well. I asked for eggs, French rolls and turkey bacon and grabbed a carton of milk on my way to eat.

I had just finished eating and taken a few steps outside when I heard the mortar rounds buzzing in the sky, coming

Mortar rounds of all kinds. They are all deadly. This collection had been buried in the ground and although some were not serviceable, they could still kill if buried with live rounds as road bombs.

toward the dining facility. The structure was nothing more than giant, flat-topped tents surrounded by three-foot tall walls of concrete. There were also bomb shelters made of concrete inside the wall to allow easy access in case of an attack. These concrete shelters were like small tunnels with no doors that people could run into from both sides.

The scariest moment was not when the bomb fell on us, but rather listening to the sound of the bomb flying in the sky: it is the sound of imminent death, death within seconds for us all. The roof of the facility was made of canvas, and the mortar round was not only heavy, but also very hot. It would go right through the roof. Everyone in or around the facility had to rush toward the shelter, and I was not too far from them. I found a place in the middle of the shelter because the ground impact would slow the fragments from flying too far. The chances of getting hit there were less than those of the people near the open door.

There were eighteen mortar rounds. All but three missed us. I later discovered that one of them injured a base commander who was immediately taken by Medivac to Baghdad. One of the rounds dug deeply into the ground next to the Marine Supply and Personnel Officer. Two of the mortars directly hit Marine supply containers and started a fire.

When it was over, I stood up and went to my tent. I found all the members of the other two teams standing in front of the tent shelter waiting for an answer from those coming from the dining facility. They were all wearing shorts and bullet-proof vests and nothing else, and their bewildered eyes were full of questions. They asked me if it was true that there was a

fire in the dining facility. At that point, I hadn't known if anyone had been injured.

The dining facility was always a target for mortar fire
during meal times. The attackers wanted to score big.
Eventually, a lot of the soldiers did not go there to eat,
preferring to ask others to bring food back for them. I knew
that we would have this risk as long as we were in this war,
so I figured what the hell — I had to have my turkey bacon
and my eggs! It was better to die with a full stomach.

I entered the tent and took my interrogation equipment
and my laptop and left. Some of the team members went back
to sleep. On my way back to my HMMWV, I heard about the
commanding officer who had been hit. The news came over my
radio. I turned on the engine and waited for it to warm up and
then drove to the command's tent complex to ask who had
been hit. It was one of the saddest moments because I found

The Beduins had more terrain-adapted tents.

out that one of our bravest and best men might lose his arm as a result of the attack.

I left to go to the gate, passing a team member who was chewing tobacco. Just inside the gate was a little local market on the base that sold local food like homemade chicken and our favorite local Iraqi bread, as well as the stolen goods from our American supply convoys. They even had Turkish and Iranian satellite dishes that rotated and could connect you to the whole world for only $110 — and free installation in the comfort of your favorite tent. My friends Abu Haydar and Mahadi were always there. They were highly educated, trained lawyers who could not find jobs in Iraq and turned to selling these things inside the base. I never involved them in my real business for the sake of their own safety, but I had visited Hamid's mother and father many times. They always made a delicious red tea for me and even fed me a dish of homemade stewed meat. Hamid had a beautiful, loving family.

I bought tobacco for one of my team members and went to meet my informant. I expected Mr. Clean to tell me where one of our worst nightmares, Abu She-Haymah, was hiding. An ordinary street sweeper for the Ministry of Municipality and Public Works, he made less than $45 per month during Saddam's time, but had gotten a contract for $30,000 U.S. from Zarqawi to plant road bombs. Abu-She was one of the major killers in our jurisdiction.

Two nights earlier, we had set him up: The Special Forces raided his house in the Gold Hill Village, but he had spent the night in Baghdad. He was the luckiest person in Iraq — had he been arrested by the Special Forces he would have gotten the death penalty. His road bombs had destroyed more than six convoys and killed more than twenty Americans. The Special Forces were able to catch members of his gang, but he had gotten away.

My informant did tell me where Abu-She was hiding. I went back to my tent and gave my team member his tobacco, then sat on my bed to write my report. Just before lunch time, I went to the Marine Command and gave them my report. After they read it, I knew they would cook up a good plan to catch Abu-She. Satisfied, I went to lunch.

That night, the dining facility had huge steaks and the biggest shrimp I had ever seen in my life. They also had enormous lobster, so I took as much as I could and a big bottle of orange juice and sat down to enjoy my meal. I didn't know it then, but that very well could have been the last meal I ever ate in my life.

After lunch, I parked my HMMWV next to my tent and went inside. I sat on top of my bed with my boots still on and laid back to relax. I fell asleep instantly when one of the team members came and tapped on my shoulder, waking me. He told me to take off my boots and go back to sleep. I sat up and looked around: nearly all of my team members were in the room. I asked them why they hadn't gone to work — why hadn't they gotten anything done. One of them told me that the senior staff had made an arrangement with the Special Forces to escort us to a nearby mosque that preached against Americans and the multinational forces.

There were three Muslim prayers left that day: one in the late afternoon and two at night. The mission was to be that night, but we had told the senior staff not to arrange night missions. I knew this was in direct violation of the command of order, but wondered whether they had called Baghdad to ask for permission. I told the team members that the senior officers might have had themselves or someone else killed for not following orders from the superior missions command. I did not know that the possibility of our own deaths waited only four hours in the future.

I took my boots off and lay on my back, folding my arms on my chest to go to sleep.

At 6 P.M. the mission convoy was lined up. The first vehicle in the line was a Marine Striker, followed by my own vehicle. Iraqi insurgents always kill the people in the second vehicle because they knew that this was the command vehicle. We have since changed this, but that day, it was too late for us. The third vehicle in line was my team's vehicle, and the fourth in line was another Marine Striker armored vehicle. Last in line was a third Marine Striker.

At one minute past six, the convoy commander gave us the order to move. A second later, the Tactical Commander asked us in the second vehicle to stop the mission because he wanted some changes made. The Tactical Commander (T.C.) of the third vehicle wanted me to command his vehicle and help to translate the speech from the local mosque's loud speaker because his English translator needed help with his English.

As a T.C. in command of the second vehicle, I was in the senior officer's place because he was standing up to hold the long range machine gun for the vehicle. The senior staff member had experience as a gunner, so now I was in the commander's seat. He took my seat and my command spot. I left my vehicle and went to the third vehicle. I sent the gunner from the third vehicle to hold the machine gun for the senior officer. All of this took less than four minutes, and the mission proceeded. We popped smoke and left a cloud of dust behind us.

We took a narrow dirt road that went under the freeway ramp. We managed to make it to Sewayrah road in a few minutes. The mission commander gave the final alert command and we focused on the road movements.

Far in the distance, I saw the mosque's minarets. It was the only building piercing the dark sky, and it had bright, shining, white lights. A few little bats were flying from the hedges near the trees.

We had no gunner now since he had left to hold the senior officer's machine gun. I told the driver to focus on the speed of the vehicle ahead of him. I was watching the right side of the road and paying attention to the command radio. The translator was directly behind me and another team member was behind the driver, watching the left side of the road. We were rocking and rolling as fast as an armored vehicle could go, our HMMWVs screeching through the night. The mosque was getting closer and closer with every second.

We were two hundred yards from the mosque when it was time to stop. Suddenly, the loudest noise I have ever heard resonated through the night: an IED went off on one of the senior officer's vehicles. There was a very bright flash and a huge cloud of smoke. I could not see the senior officer's

Our team truck after the road bomb (IED) had finished with it.

vehicle through the thick clouds of smoke.

I was alert to what was going on and felt very apprehensive. Time had stopped: I thought, "Oh no! Oh no!" I glanced at my watch and pressed the button for the light, illuminating the terrified reactions of the senior staff vehicle and its passengers. It was 6:18:11 P.M.

I looked at my driver and patted him on the shoulder, then told him to back up as fast as he could. There is a standing order to back off immediately in the case of a road bomb's detonation, allowing troops to see the enemy clearly and to fight back. It also enables troops to move away from the kill zone. The driver pumped the gas and the HMMWV screamed like hell away from the site.

The second road bomb designated to go off on my vehicle was to be detonated by a remote control, but thankfully,

There were holes all over the ammo cans which were in the trunk.

Our pride, the Tombstone outlaw's ghost.

it didn't go off because whoever had wired it had done it incorrectly, connecting the hot wire that was supposed to go to the charge to the remote receiver by mistake, burning the remote's receiver instead of igniting the charge.

The Convoy Command ordered a one-hundred yard retreat and instructed us to dismount from our fighting positions. We did so, and then exited the armored vehicles to fight the enemy. Only 45 seconds had passes since the road bomb detonated on the senior staff. I spotted an extended cab pick-up truck driving fast toward the bamboo across the canal. It was far from the M16 range, so I told the Marine Striker to shoot the junior truck that was passing over the little bridge. He struggled with his gun a bit, and then asked me again while he was looking in the direction of the pick-up. It was too late, though: Rayid Hussein, the driver of the pick-up who had

detonated the two bombs, had disappeared through the night and gone back to Jebalah, a town about ten miles from where we were.

Sheik Goodman had heard the news of the road bombs. Two days later, he came and told me Rayid Hussein's name.

Senior staff had survived the road bombs, but his back was injured from the impact. He was immediately taken to the hospital by Medivac, and the mission was cancelled. My HMMWV was totaled. Luckily, it had been one of the new armored vehicles, or we could have all died.

Later, the senior officer was told by the command in Baghdad that he would personally be held responsible if he left the base in any mission after five P.M.

The next day, I designated different tasks to my team members and restricted their activity specifically to intelligence collection. No more night missions.

The next morning, Sheik Goodman called me and told me that he was sorry for what had happened to my team and requested to see me the following day. I told him that he was always welcome. He said that he would give me the names and locations of all those involved in the attack, and I told him I was all ears. Sheik Goodman did come the next day, and he gave me more than I expected.

Sheik Goodman came on time as he had promised. He parked his white pick up a hundred yards from the gate in the visitors designated area.

He left his armed guard watching his pickup as usual. Soon as he left, each one of them had slung his AK 47 on his shoulder. They both held cigarettes and stood by the side of the pickup talking to each other.

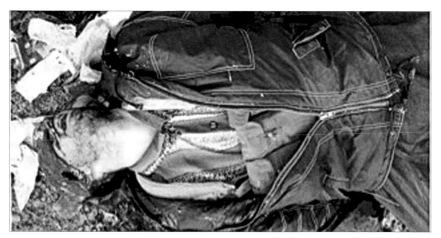

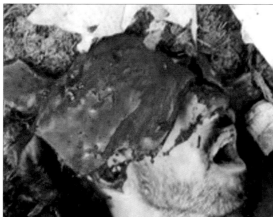

Road bomb victim shows what a road bomb (IED) did to a human skull.

BELOW:
Another bomb result on the Death Highway. Only the feet were left intact.

This is the Death Highway. It is in the middle of the Death Triangle of Baghdad, Hillah and Fallujah. Close to 70% of us died traveling through this freeway at some point.

Sheik Goodman fixed his huge sheik golden gown (*Ebayah*)) and started walking toward the gate. It is good that he was always on time because I was parked not too far from the gate and was waiting for his arrival.

I waved at the gate guards to let him in. He saluted the guards and entered. I left my HMMWV and walked towards him. We reached each other halfway and we hugged as two brothers who had missed each other for too long. He told me that he was glad to see me alive. I told Sheik Goodman that God's justice was stronger than their mockery and sneaky work.

We reached my special tent and I prepared two cold Cokes for us. I gave him one and opened the other. Then he sat on the chair next to my single table and I sat on my regular chair. He asked me how it had happened. I told him the whole story with the exception of the reason for the mission. It was sad that any of us died in a mission that could have been avoided by adjusting to a better plan than the night plan which gave the enemy more of an advantage. It was also sad that if anyone had to die in that mission, it couldn't only have been the two people who coordinated it with the special force.

Goodman told me to start writing. He also told me that he would give me the big fish of the IED-making ring. He said that Ali Mama was the head of the snake and I had to cut the head off the snake to prevent it from biting. I totally agreed with him and the name Ali Mama gripped my attention. Ali is a man's name and Mama being attached to it is kind of funny. I asked the sheik why Ali was called Ali Mama. The sheik did not take a second before he waved his hand in a manner that explained it all. Then he told me that Ali had been a soft boy when he was little, therefore he was given the name Ali Mama. Psychologically I understood why Ali Mama was doing what he was doing now. I told the sheik that Ali was one of the most dangerous "soft men" in my world right now, and I had to find his "soft self" and keep him behind bars.

Goodman told me that Reiyad Hussein, who had a grain selling shop five hundred yards from the IED site that hit my HMMWV two nights ago, was a small fish. He detonated both bombs and drove away in his white Nissan pickup truck to Jebala village ten miles away from Dolaimy, where both IEDs were planted on the road. As soon as he mentioned the pickup

I knew he was right. I had seen the extended cab junior truck leaving but it was too dark to see the color.

Goodman told me that Ali Mama, who lived in Baghdad on Palestine Street, was the person I should go after because he was not only the major maker of IEDs, but he also taught how to make the IEDs for ten U.S. dollars a person. He told me that Ali Mama's private school was located in his house, but he didn't know more than that. Later I sent one of my informants to downtown Baghdad and he located Ali Mama's school in Saddamiyat Al Kharkh. I sent the report to the special force in his area through the necessary channel.

Goodman told me that the mokhtar Muhammad AL Essawi's brother in Mahmodyah also has an IED making school for ten dollars a person and his school was between his brother's house and Mohammad Ali Thayer's grocery store in Mahodyah. I also sent one of my informants to locate the mokhtars who lived near Mohammed's grocery store and to find his brother's school. My informant found both the mokhtar and the brother and the information was sent to Mahmodyah base Special Forces through the necessary channel.

Goodman told me that brothers Shinars Ghalibb and Nasie Shinars were both former colonels in the Saddam Fidayeen, which was the suicidal force that wore explosives belts and were seen during the parades of the former Saddam. They were special forces and suicidal. They had a school in Mahmudayh along Baghdad Hillah freeway next to the Nurah Adel Al Torty grocery shop, not too far from where Al Askan street intersected with Baghdad Babylon freeway in

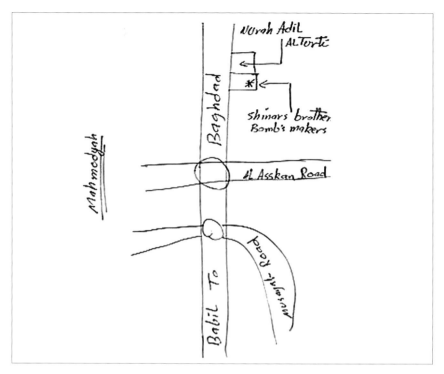

Brother Shinar, the advanced remote controlled (IED) maker's location in Mahmodyah, south Baghdad.

Mahmodyah. Sheik Goodman told me that the Shinars not only made remote detonated IEDs but they also made advance IEDs that work with beam devices. He said that the Shinars brothers sold and made IEDs for whomever paid the most. I sent one of my informants to locate the Shinars brothers' school and the information was also sent to the Mahmodayh base through the necessary channels.

Goodman told me that he had done with the IED ring but there were special important characters we, the Americans, needed to capture and take to justice. I told Goodman to go ahead and tell me who they were.

Goodman straightened himself in his chair and told me that Hajji Atradd Ebbrah, who lived in the Mahaweel jurisdiction, not too far from Hillah, had attacked seven American supply convoys and taken eight eighteen wheelers. Seven of the eighteen wheelers were licensed in his name and he operated them on Hillah Baghdad freeway. All eight eighteen wheelers had the number 1.500 written on their special plates. Hajji Atradd was driving one of them in Hafar Al Batten between the Saudi and Iraq borders. Hajji Atradd was then in Hillah Hospital because he had been attacked by some of his gang's members by mistake. Goodman told me that Hajji Atradd and his son Khalid, who formerly lived in Jordan, were now local celebrities for attacking the American convoys. He told me that Khalid lived in Mahmodyah, and presently had the biggest gang in the area that specialized in attacking the convoys between Fallujah Mahmoday Baghdad.

Goodman mentioned a man named Nizar the butcher who contracted with the Americans to supply the Mahmodyah base with local meat. Nazar, he said, had betrayed the American trust. I asked Goodman to tell me about it.

Ahmed Chalabi had betrayed the trust of President Bush. He told me that Nizar was financing the gangs who put IEDs on Hillah Baghdad freeway and also killed and beheaded the Iraqi local translators who worked for the Americans.

Finally Goodman told me that in May, 2003, Hajji Morewan, who lived in Tell Al Zahab between bridge seventeen and bridge twenty-one, on the eastern side of Hillah Baghdad freeway, had shot dead all the Americans when their helicopter forcibly landed on Tell Al Zahab and then escaped to Syria, where he was still today.

An urgent report had been sent by me to the chain of command. I knew that the killing had taken place a year and a half ago but Hajji Morewan had never been known to us. Now the warrant officers' souls might rest in peace.

Sheik Goodman said to me, "Find them," and then he left. I never saw him again. I never even got the opportunity to shake hands with him and say goodbye. I was told to go to Hillah to interview a local translator who worked for Kellogg, Brown, and Root, an American company that contracted with the Department of Defense to provide local services. It was a good surprise that allowed me to meet my former crew in Hilah and also to see the historical Babylon.

13

LAST TRIP TO BABYLON

Extremely high risk mission. In the last two weeks we had had two convoys attacked and destroyed. Screening was not my main work; I had more than my hands full. Screening was part of the civilian company, Kellogg Brown and Roots's job. Sometimes we would fill in for them when they had a shortage of screening staff in the area. Sometimes their screening staff preferred not to go if it was extremely risky or if they didn't have an escort. Then — here we go — send the intelligence guys. They thought we were invincible or immortal or something. But we were made of flesh and bone and we also died. We had children like every-one else, children we missed, who would cry if we died. We also had feelings, but we were trained to hide them. We cried inside without tears.

Babylon's only remaining gate, the Ishtar Gate, one of the eight gates of the inner city of Babylon, was built during the reign of Nebuchadnezzar II (604 – 562 B.C.).

Six o'clock, the convoy was on the road and we had left the usual cloud of dust behind us. We took the back road and merged with the Babylon Baghdad road eight miles later. I had mixed feeling about seeing my former friends in Babylon and also realized that this could be my last trip alive. The freeway is infested by IEDs. I was more worried because I now knew that Nizar, who was financing the IED road planters, was working with *us* in Mahmodyah and he knew our movements from Mahmodyah to the others cities. After all, Nizar hated the translators and I was going to qualify some of them for jobs. One thing made me comfortable: Nizar did not work at the same base with me, otherwise I would have known for a fact that he would kill some of us today.

When we hit the freeway we pumped the HMMWV's

large engines and they screamed like hell. We were rocking and rolling towards Babylon like a rocket in the sky heading for the moon. Soon we reached the first freeway checkpoint. The guards opened the road and waved us to pass. We waved back and were gone. The second checkpoint came and went. Soon I saw on the far horizon, a huge palace. It was foggy but the high sky-piercing palace was clear. I knew then that we were a few minutes from Babylon. The driver told me that he saw the palace. I told him to focus on the road because we would go to see the palace later, after the mission was done.

We reached the assigned location. We found every person involved ready to have his part of the job finished. Therefore our mission didn't last too long before the happy translator shook hands with us and said good bye.

Babylon is still a beauty, but it was foggy that day.

My heroes — the brave U.S. Marines, who fearlessly escorted us everywhere.

Most of the crew had gone to see the Babylonian museums. I went to look for my former crew. I thought the dining facility was a place to start looking for them, since it was lunchtime. It was the perfect idea. I had put one step into the food line in the dining facility when my friend 1st Lieutenant Burbank screamed my name. Then he said, "What the heck are you doing here? Who is going to die?"

I told Burbank that the guy who hurt 1st Luieutenant Travis was going to die because we had just helped in hiring some people to go after him. We hugged like brothers. We sang together a special song that had meant a lot to us since we had been in the U.S. I hugged and shook hands with about fourteen people in the dining facility food line. The Romanians were totally shocked and surprised to see a huge number of troops hugging and talking loudly, like never before, in the dining facility. I thought the Romanians would understand later.

I filled my plate with food, followed Burbank and sat down with him at the far table that he likes most. The dining facility was packed. It was a true concrete building, not like our tent dining facility. Mortar rounds would not stand a chance of damaging it. It would take ten surface-to-surface rockets to bring it down. I felt comfortable sitting and eating without worry for once. We talked about many different things . . . Lieutenant Travis' death and how many times he came close to having his head blown up by a sniper round. I told him about the IED that had almost taken my life four days ago.

We finished our plates and left the dining facility. He offered to show me around and I asked him to show me how to get to the Babylon King Museum. I knew he was busy and I

The location of Saddam's palace in Babylon was brilliantly chosen on the shore of the Euphrates.

had only a few minutes to squeeze in the museum visit. He pointed to three buildings next to the majestic palace that Saddam Hussein had built on the top of the highest hill by the Euphrates River. The palace's huge windows and pillars, decorated with white ceramic and love poems, are the main feature of it's beauty. The palace's gold color was semi-blinding because of the fog that was slowly passing through the high hill. The fog also resembled a huge transparent white silk robe covering the hill. The different rose-colored jasmine trees that surrounded the palace were planted in line after line, becoming a garden of jasmine trees. I thought that Saddam wanted to link his imagination to the Babylonian king Nebuchadnezzar — or perhaps he thought that he could do better than Nebuchadnezzar. I was impressed by how beautifully the palace was located next to the museum.

I shook hands with Lieutenant Burbank, said goodbye and went to the museum. I had parked my HMMWV outside the huge museum gate. The gate was beautifully decorated by the Babylonians. There is a fox-like or a dog-like animal drawn all over the gate.

I entered the museum and saw a man wearing a white shirt and eyeglasses sitting far away behind a huge desk. I waved at him and turned to my right. Many other people were scattered in front of the pictures of their choice. It was very quiet for a museum, I knew I had little time and had to see as much as I could within twenty minutes.

I quickly pased from picture to picture. With every picture I became more fascinated and wished I had more time to spend. I felt the difference between the Iraquis in the Babylonian times and the present day Iraqis. The Babylonians were sensitive and beauty-loving human beings. Today's Iraquis are full of hate for each other and behead each other in the middle of the streets with no mercy or dignity. I wondered what had happen during the centuries to turn a highly civilized nation into groups of mass murderers, rapist and beheaders.

Finally I reached the man at the table. I saluted him and told him that I loved everything that I had seen. I told him that everything was beautiful beyond description. Then I asked him, why don't I see any of the beautiful roses and trees in Iraq today that the ancient city of Babylon had? Why did I see only palm trees everywhere and a few jasmine trees, like the kind surrounding Saddam's new palace?

He told me that his name was Khalid and he was the director general of all Babylonian museums. He told me that all the roses and different plants that I saw in their pictures were brought from the eastern mountains of Turkey where ancient Kurdistan had existed.

I asked Khalid why the Babylonians troubled themselves to go that far to find the roses rather than decorate their city with something that grew naturally in the area.

Khalid smiled, then asked me politely if I knew about why the city of Babylon was built. I answered that I had taken modern European history in high school but had not taken Middle Eastern history; otherwise I would have known why Babylon was built. Khalid smiled again and told me that the reason Babylon was built was not in the history books but resulted from a love story that had been told by the grandmothers and grandfathers to children throughout the centuries. The only two love stories I knew were Romeo and Juliet and Ghais and Layla. Romeo in Europe and Ghais in the desert of the Arab Island. I told Khalid that I would like to know the love story that had left behind this legacy of beauty that never died.

"There was a Kurdish king name Dara," Khalid began. "Dara was a wise old man who lived in his great kingdom that fell, in modern days, in the area that stretched from the Eastern mountains of Turkey to the western part of the Mediterranean Sea towards Lebanon. Dara had a strong army to protect his kingdom, but the Assyrians in the southwest were always attacking his western border. Dara, the wise man, came up with a partially evil plan. He thought that if he could make the young and strong king of Babylon, Nubba, marry his young and beautiful daughter Omade, Nubba would be his son-in-law and Nubba would then stop the Assyrian attacks on his kingdom in the west. He invited Nubba to see his kingdom and to meet his beautiful daughter, Omade. Dara was worried about what he should do if Omade did not like Nubba or Nubba did not like Omade. Dara also felt that his daughter's beauty would be enough to make Nubba's heart fall for her. Dara did not know that Nubba was also beautiful and extremely handsome.

"Nubba accepted the invitation and, to the surprise of ,everyone, Omade and Nubba fell in love at first sight. They fell in true love, and king Dara was overjoyed to see that his sinful idea had turned out to be a true love story.

"Nubba married Omade and took her with him to Babylon. Nubba also stopped the Assyrian attacks on his father-in-law's kingdom.

"Omade gave the young king Nubba three children. But she missed the mountains and the mountains' spring, the roses and the flowers. She began to go to her father's kingdom every spring to see the roses blossoms and to breathe the thin rose-saturated fresh mountain air.

"King Nubba loved Omade very much and he couldn't stand to be without her for one day. He came up with the idea of building the mountain for her in Babylon so she would stay with him in the spring. Then he built Babylon for Omade and Omade never left him again. Eventually they both died and left Babylon as a testimony of their true love until today. "

As I left Khalid I wondered why such a beautiful love story wasn't better known. I believed that the historians sometimes chose the only facts that suited them and ignored others that could have changed the course of history.

Babylon was built for Omade and the whole world had known of Babylon but not of Omade. The Kurdish owned the whole region and for two thousand years were left wandering in the peninsula without identity or attachment until today, when they have gotten a strip of what they once owned.

I have always wondered what the word "justice" really means in our world today. I left Babylon for Alexandria in order to pack and leave for the United States.

14

WEAPONS OF MASS DESTRUCTION LAB

One day before I left my job site for Baghdad to catch my flight to the U.S., one of my interrogators came running to me. I asked him what he wanted. He replied that Mr. Tollman, the informant I had introduced to him last week, did not want to talk to him anymore, but wanted to talk to me about a very important matter. From my former experience, I knew that some informants stopped working with us because they did not like an interrogator's style, personality, or they just felt more comfortable with another person.

I asked my colleague when Mr. Tollman wanted to see me. He said that Mr. Tollman was waiting for me now at the gate. I was packing to go home. I told him not to worry, that I would go to see him. I dressed and went to the gate. On my way I radioed the guard to search Tollman thoroughly. I didn't need a suicide on my last day there. Soon the guard radioed me that it was all clear. I stopped my HMMWV by the gate, saluted Tollman and took him to my interrogation tent. I had not seen him since the week before. I gave him a Coke and opened one for myself, explaining that I was leaving the next day to return to my family in the U.S. He wished me a safe arrival home.

Then Tollman said that his reason for coming that day was that he knew I would be leaving the next day and he did not want to tell anyone else what he wanted to tell me.

"I am honored to hear what you want to say," I replied.

Tollman announced that he was one of the Iraqi chemical warfare warrant officers who witnessed the gas attack on Halabshah, the Kurdish town between Iraq and Iran. He told me that the weapons of mass destruction were not all a lie; that although no nuclear weapons had been made by Saddam, there was a different gas weapon that had been made in the chemical warfare lab in Jarf Al Naddaff in Baghdad.

Tollman had told me that in May of 2003 "General Hussein" (Note the name is not correct to protect the general's identity), from the Iraqi Army chemical warfare department, had given the American colonel from 101 U.S. Army unit, two poisonous gas rockets. The rockets were three yards long, filled with a gas similar to the gas that was manufactured in the WMD lab in Jarf Al Naddaf. Tollman reported that he and General Hussein had driven on Musaib, Jarf Al Sakker's road to a cemetery next to the chemical project number 195 in Jarf Al Sakker, and given Colonel Shawn the two chemical warhead long rockets that were buried in the cemetery at that time.

I asked Warrant Officer Tollman to tell me exactly where in Baghdad the chemical lab was located. I wanted to get to the end of the story of the WMD once and for all. Why had Tollman involved me in the WMD on my last day? Why hadn't he meet with me when I first came to Iraq, when he could have made me the happiest trooper?

Tollman said that the WMD lab sat in the basement of a seven-story building on Al Ghadisyah Street in Jarf Al Naddaff, Baghdad. The building was located next to a vehicle maintenance company on Al Ghadisyah Street, not too far from the river, in the exact location between the road that comes from Al Nosor Square to intersect with Al Ghadisyah Street and the road that comes from Al Nosor Square and intersects with Al Ghadisyah Street on the river side. Tollman had a map for me, mentioning that the lab building was the tallest building on the block.

I asked Tollman if he could bring General Hussein of chemical warfare to see one of my friends since I would be leaving the next day for the U.S. He replied that he could bring General Hussein any time if I would be here, but if he had to bring General Hussein to see a person other than me, he had to first talk to that person. I assured Tollman that my friend would treat both of them just the way I treated him now. Tollman replied that life had taught him not to trust people before he knew them better. Then he told me that he and the general could be killed, in an instant, for having met with the Americans. I told Tollman that I really appreciate his patriotism and bravery. Tollman promised to bring General Hussein to talk to my friend if I liked.

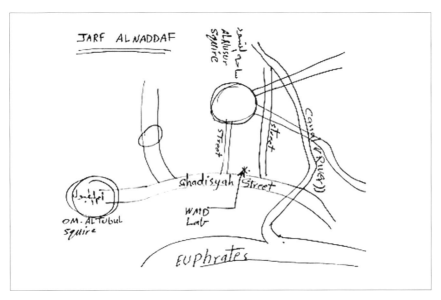

Location of Saddam's WMD Test Lab in Jarf Al Naddaf in Baghdad.

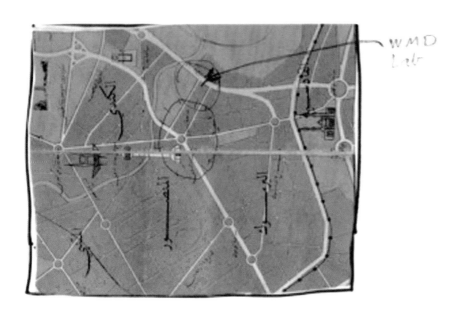

"I would like that very much and I will let my friend contact you this week."

Mr. Tollman had finished two packs of cigarettes during our conversation. He had been so carried away telling the story that he burned cigarette after cigarette. I do not smoke and I had three cartons of Rothmans in my tent, sent to me by good Americans like the people from Pittsburgh, Pennsylvania who sent food, books, personal hygiene items and cigarettes to the troops in Iraq.

I asked Tollman if I could give him a gift without him considering it a payoff for the noble job he had just done for the love of humanity. "That would be fine," he answered.

I went to my tent and and returned with three cigarette packs which I gave him, saying, "There are no words in the

This was how we lived in tent towns in the middle of nowhere with no protectiton from the flying death mortar rounds.

The holes in the sandbags were the result of mortar round fragments that had fallen from the roof into the tent.

world that I can use to thank you or to express my deep appreciation for telling me where the poison gas lab is located."

I shook hands with him and went back to my tent, where I prepared a special report about the poisonous gas lab location. I also suggested that a special interrogator should be immediately assigned to finish the case with Mr. Tollman and General Hussein. Later in Baghdad, I showed the Tollman drawing of the lab location to the commander.

The next day at 6:30 A.M. I departed for Baghdad. I woke up at 5 A.M. and went to the dining facility for the last time to have my favorite turkey bacon, eggs and milk. At 6:15 I was making the final check on my work equipment on the load truck. At 6:17 the rockets came screaming through the sky towards the base. I ran as fast as I could to the concrete shelter, seventy-five yards away. I am a fast runner, but how could I outrun a bullet? The first rocket plunged on the ground two hundred yards behind me. In a few seconds I was in the concrete shelter but I felt that I had been running forever. Those seventy-five yards were the longest distance I had ever run in my life. The screaming death was flying in the sky and my hope for life and to see my children had motivated me, made me smoke the seventy-five yards within a few seconds. Nine rockets had shaken the ground just thirteen minutes before my departure. One rocket was twenty yards from my former sleeping tent. Luckily, the rocket hit the concrete wall and missed the Ukrainian guys who were in the laundry RV six yards from the concrete wall.

It was a bad day. With God's grace no one was injured. The nine rockets had missed the people but one of them had burned a Marine supply container. Thirteen minutes later we were on the road. With no fear in our hearts,we made it to Baghdad by eight A.M.

We reported to the command and went to our new home away from home, our final transitional tents at the Baghdad International Airport. At 9:45 we were attacked again by nine rockets. I was far away from any bomb shelter. In this case, the best defense was to lay flat on your stomach next to anything that could shield your body and to leave the rest to God. That's what I did, I laid flat on my stomach next to the sandbags that surrounded the tent. Two were injured and medivaced to the hospital in Baghdad.

It was a bad day. I thought that the gangs had gotten the

The sunset in the desert town was always spectacular.

word that a big group of intelligence personnel were leaving Iraq that day so they were attacking every base.

At 10:00 that night I was tightly strapped into my seat in a C130. I looked at my watch and squeezed the light to see the time. It was 10 P.M. all right. The C130 started rolling on the strip in the dark, sprinting like a cheetah chasing a young antelope.

In a few seconds we went roaring into the sky. The jetton canisters were ignited. (Jetton is special fuel that helps a C130 climb faster on short runway strips.) The C130 pointed its nose straight up. Two young soldiers strapped into their seats in front of me started to scream in fear. I told them to be quite. The C130 suddenly and violently turned to the left and every one was thrown against the wall of the plane on his back. The two soldiers screamed even louder than before. Again, I told them to be quiet. The C130 kept repeating the same motion again and again, climbing higher and higher in a circular motion. It suddenly turned its nose down and flew steady. The two soldiers stopped screaming. Two other men next to me started gagging as if they were going to vomit. I was fine. I had seen the C130 taking off before at Baghdad International Airport. The reason the C130, and the rest of the civilian flights that contracted with the army, did that was to avoid getting shot down.

The two soldiers had calmed down and both had closed their eyes, pretending to be asleep. I knew they were just embarrassed about the screaming they had done. Ten minutes into the flight towards Kuwait, I checked my watch again and said to myself, "Home sweet home, here I come!"

Two hours later we landed at an undisclosed airport in Kuwait and changed flights for Washington, USA.

What happend in Iraq — the good, the bad, and the ugly — has become a memory buried deeply in my soul.

May God bless America, the land of the brave and the free.